Kath Cope

New Life in Nepal

DayOne

© Day One Publications 2016

First printed 2016

ISBN 978-1-84625-520-5

All Scripture quotations are from the **New International Version** 1984
Copyright © 1973, 1978, 1984

Published by Day One Publications
Ryelands Road, Leominster, HR6 8NZ

TEL 01568 613 740 FAX 01568 611 473

email—sales@dayone.co.uk

UK web site—www.dayone.co.uk

Designed by **documen**
Printed by TJ International

Chapter one:
OWN GOAL!

David watched in dismay as the ball that had hit him on the shoulder deflected into the back of the net. An own goal! He clasped his head in his hands and dropped to his knees.

A hand grabbed him roughly by the collar. 'UP!' yelled Joel, the team captain. 'Get up! No time for dramatics! Five minutes left! Come on, we've got to score!'

David staggered to his feet and glanced across to where Dad was standing, waving his arms and shouting wildly, 'Keep going! Put it behind you!'

But David couldn't put it behind him; the memory of the ball thudding into the net haunted him until the referee blew the final whistle. To his horror, tears pricked his eyes as his teammates headed off the pitch. Nobody spoke to him. Nobody patted him on the shoulder and said it didn't matter. The worst thing was that he knew it did matter. He'd let everybody down.

Dad was waiting with his kitbag. 'Happens to everyone at some time, son, don't worry. Nobody blames you.'

David miserably pulled his tracksuit top over his head. 'They all blame me,' he said. 'They think I'm a loser. Sam as good as said it.'

'I'm sure he didn't mean that. Now, how about having a drink and biscuit with the boys?' asked Dad, nodding his head towards where most of the team had gathered around Ronnie, their coach, their heads close together. Certain that they were talking about him, David shook his head. 'No. I just want to go home.'

'It might be better to face them now,' suggested Dad, 'get it over with. It won't seem as bad tomorrow, and I can promise you that you'll be able to laugh about it one day. I once got sent off ...'

But David had already started walking across the field to the car park. He'd heard all about Dad being sent off in a football game for picking up the ball and running round the pitch with it when he thought the referee had blown the whistle for half-time. The story usually made him laugh, but not today. He couldn't believe he would ever recover from the humiliation of this match.

Chapter two:
UNEXPECTED NEWS

When David and Dad arrived home, Mum and Emily were in the kitchen. David could see immediately that something was up as they exchanged that special look they used when they had a secret. Dad must have noticed it too, because he asked, 'What are you two up to?'

'You'll never guess what's happened!' said Mum with a huge smile.

'They never will!' squealed Emily, as she hopped from foot to foot. 'So can I tell them? Please? Please?'

'Go on then, tell us!' shouted David. 'Get on with it! What's happened?'

'Uncle Richard and Auntie Sophie have got a baby!'

The surge of excitement that had briefly bubbled in David's stomach disappeared as quickly as it had arrived. 'A baby?' he echoed. 'How can they have got a baby? She's never been pregnant.'

Emily tutted and gave him a look that suggested he was a total idiot.

'A baby girl,' continued Mum. 'Uncle Richard's sent an email this morning. He says they're going to call her Rachel. She's just a few months old and apparently her poor mum died very soon after she was born. It's very sad, but someone's asked Uncle Richard and Auntie Sophie if they'll take care of her until they can find a couple who'd be willing to adopt her. And the really exciting thing is that Uncle Richard says they themselves would be very interested in adopting her if it's possible! Oh, I can't believe it, a baby! They'll make such wonderful parents!'

David had never seen Mum so excited; Dad was laughing and begging her to slow down so that he could understand what she was saying; and Emily was dancing round the room. It seemed to David that he was the only one who wasn't hysterical with excitement.

'They sent a photo!' shrieked Emily. 'She's totally gorgeous—come and look!' She raced to the laptop and clattered the keys until the screen filled with a photograph of a leafy garden in Nepal and the well-loved faces of their auntie and uncle who had been missionaries there for three years.

Dad studied the photograph of Auntie Sophie cradling a baby wrapped in a pink blanket with Uncle Richard looking over her shoulder at the tiny face peeping out at the world.

'So, it seems we've got a new little girl in the family! How about that, David?' Dad said at last.

'It's not the same when you don't get to see them, though, is it?' moaned David. 'Sometimes it feels as if Uncle Richard and Auntie Sophie aren't in our family any more, never mind a baby we've never seen.' He picked up his football kit. 'I'm going to have a shower.'

'But you haven't looked at Rachel!' cried Emily. 'He never even looked at the photo,' she wailed to her parents.

As he headed for the stairs, David heard Dad say, 'I'm sure he'll look when he's had a shower. He was a bit fed up after the game this morning. Guess what happened ...'

The voices faded as David reached the top of the stairs and he was spared the humiliation of hearing Dad relate the story of the own goal. He stuffed his football kit into the washing basket, threw his bag in the corner of his bedroom and flopped down onto his bed. This was the worst day of his life. First the football match, and now news of his uncle and auntie adopting a baby in Nepal. If they had a little girl to love and look after on the other side of the world, they might never come home.

After a while, he heard someone coming up the stairs, so he jumped up from his bed, raced into the bathroom and turned the key in the lock. He glanced at his reflection in the bathroom mirror: the face that looked back at him was still spattered with mud. He touched the spot that was threatening to erupt on the side of his nose. 'Rubbish!' he snarled, 'everything's rubbish!' and tearing off his clothes he stepped into the shower.

'The water board've just phoned to say you've used all the water in the reservoir!' called Dad about ten minutes later as he hammered on the bathroom door. 'Time to come out! Mum says lunch is almost ready.'

David had hardly got through the kitchen door when Emily shouted, 'Are you going to look at this photo or not, David?'

Perhaps if she'd not sounded so bossy he would have looked; instead, he picked up the newspaper and went straight to the table and sat down.

'Is lunch ready?' he asked, leafing through the sports section of the Saturday paper. 'Only I was hoping to go round to Ben's this afternoon. They've got a new puppy, and I said I'd go and have a look at it.'

'You haven't looked at Rachel yet!' protested Emily indignantly. 'You're more interested in Ben's dog than in our new cousin!'

David pretended he was absorbed in the article he was reading so he didn't have to answer; he carried on reading the paper until Mum told him to put it away. Then he ate lunch without engaging in any of the conversation around the table, and asked to be excused as soon as he'd finished.

Chapter three:
DISAPPOINTMENT

David had been dreading going back to school on Monday and facing the rest of the team, but by the end of the day they were united in a protest about the amount of history homework they'd been given. Most of his friends didn't really blame him for the football defeat, and even Sam eventually stopped teasing him about it after a few days. He scored in their next game and life seemed back to normal—apart from the fact that there seemed no end to the flow of photographs from Nepal. Auntie Sophie sent long reports of how many hours Rachel was sleeping at night and, it seemed to David, details of every time she coughed or smiled.

'Uncle Richard emailed this morning to say they're postponing their leave,' announced Mum one evening as she was dishing out the vegetables. 'They've got to be available to go to meetings about the adoption.'

'I was so looking forward to them coming home!' moaned Emily. 'How long's it going to take?'

'They've no idea,' said Mum. 'I expect there are a lot of things to sort out. We'll have to wait and see.'

David hadn't even tried to hide his disappointment when the email arrived to say that the adoption could take many months.

He hated it at church when people talked to him about Nepal.

'You must feel really blessed to have your uncle and auntie out on the mission field,' boomed Mr Shepherd one morning as David was waiting for his parents to stop talking to the pastor.

'It's quite hard actually,' replied David as politely as he could. 'Sometimes it feels like we'll never see them again.'

Mr Shepherd was clearly surprised by David's answer and didn't seem to be able to think of anything to say other than a quiet, 'Oh!'

When David continued to say, 'It was a bit sad on Christmas Day last year—just us four and Grandad. We really miss them at family occasions.' Mr Shepherd muttered, 'Oh' again and suddenly found, to David's relief, that he needed to go and talk to someone else!

Even the youth group wanted to talk about Rachel, and thanks to Emily they knew every detail of how she was getting on. Even if David had wanted to talk about her, there was nothing left to say. He'd tried to start a conversation with Lucy Metcalf by chatting about Rachel, but she'd only replied, 'Yeah, Emily told me all about that.' And then he'd felt very stupid—his chances of impressing Lucy were greatly diminished, and he'd fallen out with Emily on the way home when he'd accused her of telling everyone all their news about Rachel.

'So what?' she snapped. 'It's not as if you're interested in her. If you were, you'd write to them or send them an email.'

'There's nothing left to say!' yelled David. 'You say it all in your emails. You must send at least ten a week!'

'What if I do?' insisted Emily. 'Auntie Sophie says she loves reading my news.'

'Well, stop sending her my news as well, and then I'd have something to say!' bellowed David, and they walked the rest of the way home in silence.

The months went by, and the football season moved towards its climax, with David's team qualifying for the finals of the league cup; although they didn't win, David scored two goals and was voted Man of the Match. The exam period came and went, the weeks of revising paid off for both children, and they were soon looking forward to the approaching summer break.

One Thursday evening, as they sat around the table, Emily said, 'Melissa Dewhurst's going to Florida in August. They're going to Disneyland and everything.'

David swallowed the food in his mouth. 'How come we never go anywhere exciting?' he grumbled.

'Well now,' answered Dad, 'it's funny you should say that, because Mum and I have been talking and we wondered if you might like to go and see Uncle Richard and Auntie Sophie?'

'In Nepal?' stammered Emily.

David put down his knife and fork and looked from one parent to the other.

'In Nepal,' confirmed Dad. 'In Pokhara, to be exact! It's all booked. In fact, we leave on 4th August! And you'll be spending your birthday with your auntie and uncle, David! That exciting enough for you?'

Even Emily was speechless at the surprising news. For a few seconds there was complete silence, during which time David thought about all the people he'd half invited to a wall-climbing event he was planning to celebrate his birthday.

'And another exciting thing,' said Mum as she stood up to clear the plates. 'We're all off to the doctor's on Monday for the first of our injections!'

Chapter four:
THE ADVENTURE BEGINS

David pressed his face against the plane window. It had been such a long flight—two flights in fact—and he hadn't slept for a second, not even when they put the lights out for about six hours. Now, just as the pilot had announced that they'd be landing in twenty minutes, he felt very tired. Across the aisle, three young Nepalese men who had joined the flight in Doha were chattering excitedly and jostling each other to look out of the window.

The deep brown ridges of the wide valley below them were broken up by splashes of green as fields and trees came into view, and then suddenly the city of Kathmandu was sprawled beneath them. David wiped the tiny window as a maze of rooftops and tangled overhead cables appeared, and he watched in fascination as every minute brought new features into focus. Soon he could see colourful buildings covered with ivy, buildings covered with shabby blue tarpaulins, and a wide meandering river full of drifting boats. A bus was chugging its way along a narrow street packed with cars—he blinked and looked again, because surely there were people sitting on the roof of the bus! Then the airport buildings flashed by and the plane juddered as the wheels hit the tarmac. David took a deep breath: somewhere very close by, his uncle and auntie were waiting for them. He couldn't wait!

The Nepalese young men were out of their seats long before the plane taxied to the arrivals gate. They were on their feet and trying to retrieve their luggage from the overhead lockers while the stewardesses shouted and pointed.

'Excited to be home, I think!' whispered Dad.

'I know how they feel,' thought David; he couldn't wait to see his family again.

It seemed to take hours to get through the airport buildings, but at last they followed the crowds of people surging through the exit and arrived in the sunshine. David scanned all the faces, looking for Uncle Richard.

David was scared he was going to be separated from the rest of his family as crowds of Nepalese people jostled around them, trying to take their cases from them and tug them towards the line of waiting taxis.

'Hold onto your bags!' yelled Dad. 'We don't know where we're going yet.'

Suddenly, there was Auntie Sophie, pushing her way through the crowd and waving madly, a black-haired toddler in her arms, and then she was hugging them and kissing Mum and Emily. Rachel looked bewildered and turned to hide her face on her mum's shoulder.

Then David realized that Uncle Richard wasn't there to meet them. The disappointment hit him like a physical punch. He hoped he didn't let it show, but Auntie Sophie seemed to sense how he was feeling because as she kissed him she said, 'Uncle Richard's gutted he couldn't come with us, David—I'm so sorry he's not here. He's been summoned to a meeting, and as he's taking next week off, he couldn't really say no. Anyway, you'll see him tomorrow.'

'Tomorrow?' mumbled David. 'Aren't we going to your house straightaway?'

'It's too far, sweetheart,' said Auntie Sophie. 'It's taken us six hours to get here, and I couldn't expect Dipendra to drive back to Pokhara tonight.' She turned slightly and they looked over her shoulder to where a man was waiting by a mud-splattered Land Rover; he responded to her wave by strolling towards them.

Rachel was now sitting happily in Mum's arms and giggling as Emily tickled her. David watched from a distance, unsure how to approach such a small child. Would she even understand what he was saying? He supposed that the look Emily gave him meant he should join in making a fuss of Rachel, but he didn't know how; so he settled for stroking her arm, and then went to help Dad and Dipendra stash their luggage on top of the Land Rover.

Dipendra drove them the short distance to the Thamel district of Kathmandu, where they were to spend the night in a small hotel. After putting their bags and cases in their rooms, Auntie Sophie took them to a pizza restaurant a few streets away. Relieved to see something as familiar as pepperoni pizza, David ate enthusiastically, and even Rachel had a slice of pizza and an ice cream. David thought how perfect the evening would have been if only Uncle Richard had been there.

'Well,' said Mum, as they walked back to their hotel, 'I didn't expect to eat pizza in Kathmandu! And the hotel has Western toilets!'

'Mum's obsessed with toilets!' laughed Emily.

'Not obsessed,' corrected Mum; 'I just need to know there'll be one!'

'By the time we come back here in a fortnight, your mum will be an intrepid adventurer!' laughed Dad, swapping Rachel from one arm to the other.

'So she might not eat a hot chilli on the plane on the way home?' asked David.

'All right, all right!' said Mum, joining in with the laughter. 'I thought it was a bean! But now I know better!'

It was dark by the time they got back to the hotel, and, although it was only 8.30 in the evening, Auntie Sophie suggested that they get an early night ready for the long journey the following day.

David lay awake for a long time staring out into the darkness and listening to the sounds in the hotel. Rachel was crying in the room next door and he supposed she was worn out with meeting her family for the first time. A clap of thunder overhead made him jump and he rolled over onto his other side, trying to blot out the sound of heavy rain lashing against the window. Kathmandu was so different from anywhere he had ever been before, and he hoped it wasn't going to rain all the time. He felt quite excited at the prospect of the six-hour journey the next day. The pizzas had been brilliant—in fact, everything had been great so far; but what meeting was so important that it delayed you coming to meet your family when you hadn't seen them for three years? It was an unhappy thought to

17

have in your mind when you were just about to go to sleep, but David couldn't help being bitterly disappointed that Uncle Richard hadn't come to meet them.

Chapter five:
AN EXCITING JOURNEY

David was still thinking about Uncle Richard's absence as they set out on their journey to Pokhara the next morning. He had been allowed to sit at the front between Dad and Dipendra. He saw the shock on Emily's face when they were surrounded by beggars, and realized he wasn't the only one who was struggling to adjust to seeing so many people dressed in rags. Even as they were about to set off, a tiny lady with a frail-looking baby on her hip held out a hand which was horribly twisted. He watched Auntie Sophie give her one or two tiny coins before she climbed into the Land Rover beside Emily.

'I know it's hard,' she explained as Dipendra carefully manoeuvred the car away from the kerb, 'but there are so many needy people, and you just can't give to everyone.'

David watched the people recede into the distance as the Land Rover picked up speed: some still had their arms outstretched towards them. He closed his eyes to shut out their sad faces.

It seemed to take forever to get through the busy city streets, where cows and rickshaws competed with cars, lorries, scooters and buses for space on the road. Ahead of them, a lorry swerved up onto the pavement to avoid a cow which lay in the middle of the road, and a lady in a blue sari, who was carrying one small child and leading another by the hand, dived into a shop doorway to get out of the way. The cow didn't move and Dipendra was also forced to mount the kerb to avoid hitting it.

'If you do any driving while you're here, John,' said Auntie Sophie, 'be really careful not to hit a cow—you'll be in ever such a lot of trouble! They're regarded as sacred here, and it's against the law to harm them.'

Dad laughed. 'Now that I've seen the roads, I can assure you I won't be driving anywhere. Anyway, you haven't got a car, have you?'

'No,' replied Auntie Sophie, 'we have an ancient motor scooter in case we need to go any distance. Mostly we walk or take the bus, so it's quite a treat to have the use of the Land Rover. Keep your eyes open for scooters with whole families on them!'

Sure enough, before long, David saw a scooter carrying two grown-ups and three small children, and within minutes another one was weaving its way between the cars, with the driver trying to hold a metal filing cabinet on the passenger seat with one hand while he steered with the other.

'Can you see the flags up there?' Auntie Sophie pointed up a street to their left. 'That's the temple where the "living goddess" lives. We haven't got time to visit today, but maybe you could go when you come back to Kathmandu in a couple of weeks. You might just see her peeping through one of the windows.'

'Is she a real goddess?' asked David, leaning as far forward as the seat belt allowed, trying to get a glimpse of the temple.

'The Nepalis think she is,' said Auntie Sophie; 'they call her the Royal Kumari of Kathmandu. She's selected from lots of other little girls and has to be very brave as well as physically perfect.'

'No point in you applying then, Em!' sniggered David.

'Ha ha, very funny!' replied Emily from the back seat. 'You'll have to learn not to take any notice of David, Rachel, he's very cheeky!'

'Dabey,' repeated Rachel.

'She knows your name already, David!' said Emily, sounding as though she was a bit jealous.

'The Kumari spends her whole life in the temple from the time she's chosen until she's a teenager; then they choose someone else and she goes back to her normal life,' continued Auntie Sophie. 'People come to ask for her blessing, even the leaders of the country. She's probably one of the most important people in Nepal.'

'How old is she?' asked Emily.

Auntie Sophie and Dipendra exchanged a few comments. It was strange to hear his aunt speaking in a foreign language, and David was impressed at how fluent she appeared to be. When Dipendra finished speaking Auntie Sophie explained what he'd said. 'Dipendra thinks she's about eight. Imagine that, Emily: living in a temple when you're only eight, and only seeing your family now and again.'

'If it means only seeing David now and again, it might be worth it!' Emily giggled. David laughed as much as everyone else, and Dipendra looked puzzled until Auntie Sophie interpreted for him, and then he joined in too.

'If you ever get to be a goddess, Em, I'll come every day just to annoy you!' joked David.

'What if they want Rachel to be the living goddess?' asked Emily, sounding worried.

'There's no chance of that,' said Auntie Sophie. 'Rachel's growing up as a Christian like us.'

Chapter six:
A LONG ROAD

Heavy traffic and the erratic behaviour of some drivers made their progress out of the city very slow. After a while they turned a corner and were met by a procession of people marching towards them blowing horns and waving flags.

'What's the parade for?' asked Emily. 'Is it a special day?'

'There's always something going on in Kathmandu,' replied Auntie Sophie. 'Doesn't matter whether you're celebrating or protesting, you just get your friends together and march down the street and make as much noise as you can!'

Eventually they were out of the city. They were now driving through a wide valley, and David could see the terraced hillsides away to their left.

'Look at those gardens!' exclaimed Mum. 'They're really beautiful! What are they growing?'

'Potatoes, vegetables, a bit of wheat, mustard and herbs. Anything, really—whatever will keep their families fed, maybe even with a bit left over to sell. In a while you'll see paddy fields,' said Auntie Sophie.

There was so much to see, it was hard to know where to look first. They passed lots of children dressed in smart uniforms on their way to school, and when Mum remarked on it, Auntie Sophie said, 'Parents here know that the real key to survival is to get a good education, and even the children realize that they are very privileged if they can go to school every day.'

'So they don't moan as much as children in England when they have to get up a bit earlier to make sure they catch the bus?' said Mum, laughing and raising her eyebrows at David, who missed the bus nearly as many times as he caught it.

'They'd think they were in heaven if they could catch a bus to school; most people walk wherever they're going,' said Auntie Sophie.

'And they all look very tidy,' remarked Mum. 'I keep telling Emily and David that you're in a better frame of mind to learn if you dress properly for school. When I was a girl, we had to wear knee-length skirts, and woe betide anybody whose tie wasn't knotted properly!'

David grinned at Emily as Mum launched into one of her favourite subjects.

'Look at that!' shouted Emily as they passed a donkey plodding along under a heavy burden of leaves and branches. 'It can't see where it's going, poor thing, and you can hardly see its legs!'

'It's a mule,' said Auntie Sophie. 'They're working animals, and if they didn't carry the heavy loads, the ladies would have to do it.'

Mum and Emily both started to object but, sure enough, before long they saw a lady almost bent double by the weight of the basket on her back.

24

'There, you see,' said Auntie Sophie, 'she's carrying rocks from the river to that site over there where they're doing some building work.'

'And she's only wearing flip-flops!' exclaimed Emily. 'What if one of the rocks dropped on her foot? Anyway, how come the ladies do all the hard work?'

'Everybody has to work very hard here in Nepal if they want to feed their children, so the women are very grateful if they can work and contribute to their family's income. You mustn't expect things to be like they are at home, Emily,' said Auntie Sophie.

'But why are the ladies doing the heavy work? What are the men doing?'

Emily's question went unanswered because the traffic in front of them was slowing down so that they could pass a lorry on its side, its cargo spilled out across the road, where many hands were helping to retrieve cartons of fruit and vegetables. Dipendra slowly navigated his way through the mayhem.

'Looks like there's been a landslide,' observed Dad, pointing away to their right, where a torrent of sludge and mud had gouged a deep gash into the hillside. 'Does that happen often?'

'All the time. Result of the monsoon, I'm afraid,' said Auntie Sophie sadly. 'Sometimes the roads are washed away completely.'

'Oh dear!' murmured Mum, and David knew that she had added something else to her worry list.

'What happens then?' asked Dad. 'How do you get from place to place?'

'You have to wait till they rebuild the road,' said Auntie Sophie, 'or walk!'

'How long would it take to get to your house from here?' asked Emily.

Auntie Sophie thought for a minute. 'Probably the best part of a week—but don't worry, it's not going to happen today. This is nothing!'

No one except Rachel spoke for quite a long time; she was oblivious of the dangers of the road and the anxieties of the grown-ups, and chattered and laughed as Emily entertained her.

'I thought there would be more mountains,' said David eventually as he looked back across another wide valley. 'I really expected to see mountains covered with snow.'

'Oh, they're there all right,' answered Auntie Sophie; 'you just can't see them because of the cloud cover. Hopefully we'll get some clear days while you're here, and then you'll see how beautiful Nepal really is. Summer's not really the best time to come to Nepal because of the monsoon.'

David turned round and faced the front. Did Auntie Sophie mean that she didn't really want them to come and stay? Was that why Uncle Richard hadn't bothered to come and meet them? He shifted uncomfortably in his seat. He hoped that his aunt and uncle had wanted them to visit and that their presence wasn't going to be a nuisance. It would be awful to feel as though they were intruding and getting in the way. Dad had nodded off and Dipendra was concentrating on the road ahead. The girls were all chattering and laughing on the back seat and, just for a moment, he felt very lonely and a long way from home.

The miles rolled by. After stopping briefly at a roadside café for a drink, David slept a little until a chorus of cheers woke him up and he saw a sign that said, 'POKHARA'. The fields were replaced by more houses, and soon they were driving down narrow streets between rows of houses and shops.

'Five minutes and we'll be there,' announced Auntie Sophie, and, sure enough, a few minutes later, Dipendra turned off the main road onto a bumpy track with big potholes and large drainage channels on either side. Finally he pulled up in front of a house with a tall gate bearing a handwritten sign. A slab of concrete acting as a bridge lay across the drain.

'Here we are—home sweet home!' said Auntie Sophie with a smile as she unbuckled her seat belt.

'What does the sign say?' asked David.

'It says "Beware of the Dog", but don't worry—the dog ran away about a year ago, and nobody's seen it since, thank goodness! It belonged to the landlord who lives on the first floor and it was a real horror!' answered Auntie Sophie. 'Rachel, here's Daddy!'

David suddenly felt nervous and a little shy. Three years was a long time: what if his uncle had changed? What if it was like meeting a stranger?

Chapter seven:
REUNITED

U ncle Richard must have been listening for the
sound of the engine approaching because he came
bounding out of the gate before they had even got out of
the Land Rover. Suddenly, everything was all right. He
was just the same—a slightly taller and younger version of
Dad, with a twinkle in his eye that made you think he was
going to tell a joke.

'Good to see you, Dave!' he exclaimed when it was
David's turn for a hug. 'I've missed our footie games, mate!
Think we've got a ball somewhere for a kickaround later
on. But first things first. Welcome to our home! Let's show
you round.'

'And let's have a cup of tea!' pleaded Mum. 'I hope
you've had the kettle on.'

The hallway of the house was very cool and Auntie
Sophie stepped out of her sandals as soon as she crossed
the threshold, explaining that they should never go into
anyone's home with their shoes on.

'People will be very offended if you take dirty shoes into
their homes,' she said as they all kicked off their shoes
and followed her into a spacious lounge with pretty blue
curtains and cushions.

A little pile of toys in one corner immediately drew Rachel's eye and she toddled off to play while the visitors had a guided tour of the house. The kitchen was scrupulously clean: it looked as though every surface had been scrubbed. Auntie Sophie explained that they had to be very careful not to leave crumbs around after they'd prepared a meal unless they wanted to have ants running all round the kitchen.

'Or mice,' added Uncle Richard; 'and in one place we lived we always had a couple of chuchundras dropping by and leaving their droppings! They get mistaken for rats but they're harmless. Even so, we'd rather they didn't move in with us.'

'And this is the water filter,' pointed out Auntie Sophie. 'It's really important that you don't drink the water unless it's been filtered first. I can promise you a day in the bathroom if you drink it unfiltered! And this is my pride and joy,' she said beaming as she opened the door of an old-fashioned fridge. 'This is the only house we've had here that's had a fridge, so it's a real luxury.'

They left the kitchen and looked in each of the bedrooms and the bathroom. 'We're very lucky to have a shower and Western toilet,' said Uncle Richard, 'but water's very precious. So try not to waste any; make sure you don't leave the taps running, and ask yourself if you really need to flush the toilet.'

'Right,' said Mum. 'Really makes you think, doesn't it, about how wasteful we are at home.'

'The thing is,' explained Auntie Sophie, 'you can't always rely on the water tanks filling up if the rains don't come when they should. Same with the electricity:

sometimes there just isn't enough if everyone's using it at the same time, so we have power cuts quite regularly. You'll soon get used to it; it's just a part of life here. We always keep the candles handy! Now what about that cup of tea we promised …'

Chapter eight:
PRESENTS

'This cake is lovely,' said Mum. 'I didn't expect to be eating cake in Nepal! How do you find time to bake?'

'Oh, it's not me,' said Auntie Sophie with a laugh; 'we have a lady who comes in every morning to work for us. I showed her how to make lemon drizzle cake and now she makes it better than I do!'

'You've got a servant?' cried Emily, the look on her face saying clearly that she didn't approve.

'Maiya isn't a servant, Emily,' explained Auntie Sophie; 'she works for us, and she's very glad to have a job and earn some money so she can feed her own family. She does the cooking and the washing and the ironing and the cleaning!'

'So what do you do all day?' asked David, realizing immediately by the look on Mum's face that he had probably sounded very rude.

'Ah, straight to the point, Dave, that's the best way!' laughed Uncle Richard. 'We'll start showing you round tomorrow, and then you can see some of the things we do.'

As soon as the cases were opened, Rachel lost interest in her toys and toddled over to investigate. She was soon the proud owner of new toys and clothes that had been sent by the people from church, and Auntie Sophie exclaimed, 'Oh, how lovely!' and 'Oh, how generous!' so many times that everyone laughed.

Rachel joined in with the laughter, clapping her hands when a brightly coloured jigsaw caught her eye. Grasping one of the pieces in her chubby little hand, she considered putting it into her mouth and then tried to cram it into one of the other pieces. She handed the two jigsaw pieces to David and looked at him expectantly. Conscious that everyone was looking at him, David smiled at her and quickly made up the jigsaw. Rachel immediately swished her hands across the pieces so that they came apart.

'Again!' she insisted, handing a couple of pieces to David.

'Ha!' laughed Uncle Richard, 'you've made a friend for life, Dave. You'll be doing that jigsaw for the rest of the day!'

Sure enough, he made the jigsaw at least ten times before being summoned to the room he was to share with Emily for the duration of their stay. They were unpacking their bags when Emily gave a piercing scream. David looked towards where she was pointing.

'It's a lizard!' she shrieked.

'It's a gecko, actually, and they're completely harmless,' said Uncle Richard from the doorway. 'I'll pop him outside, though I can assure you he'll be back!'

Chapter nine:
EXPLORING

All David's doubts and anxieties had evaporated by the time he woke up the next morning. It was great to be all together as a family again, and there was no sense that they were unwelcome or intruding. He put yesterday's worries down to all the travelling and lack of sleep, and began to look forward to exploring Pokhara.

It was strange to have a shower before you went to bed rather than when you got up, but Uncle Richard had explained that the solar panels on the roof heated the water throughout the day and so the best time to shower was at night. 'But two minutes each, that's all—or the last person gets cold water, and seeing as we're the hosts, that'll be me!'

They were still eating breakfast when the sound of a bird chirruping filled the house. 'It's only the doorbell!' laughed Auntie Sophie, looking at their surprised faces before she chased after Rachel, who was running towards the front door. They returned a few minutes later with a very tiny lady in a neatly pressed orange sari.

'This is Maiya, everyone,' said Auntie Sophie, and the lady glanced round at them quickly before looking down shyly, putting her hands together and whispering, '*Namaste.*' Encouraged by a nod from Uncle Richard, they all followed his example, and put their hands together too and responded, '*Namaste*.' Auntie Sophie spoke to Maiya in her own language, and Maiya then looked up and smiled at them before bowing again and disappearing into the kitchen.

Although you could hardly tell that Maiya was there, David was glad when it was time to leave the house for a tour of the town. He was used to their home being constantly full of people from church, but he felt very uncomfortable about having someone doing his washing and cooking for him.

'I can't see the problem,' chuckled Mum, having seen his troubled look. 'You're already used to having a servant at home ... ME!'

David tried to explain, but he wasn't sure she really understood when he said it wasn't the same—but it did make him think about how he just assumed Mum would look for his school shirt when he forgot to put it in the wash, and how he took it for granted that she did the lion's share of cooking and cleaning. When he mentioned it to Emily later, she said coldly, 'I hope you're not suggesting that it's down to me to do more! I think we've heard enough about ladies doing all the work, thank you very much!'

The town was full of surprises, the main one being that the locals were so interested in them. Everywhere they went, they were followed by a small group of people who crowded in close when they were talking, as if they could understand their conversations.

'It'll be worse when we go to Beni next week—they hardly ever see foreigners there,' said Uncle Richard cheerfully as they turned into the path leading to his office. Inside, they were greeted warmly by other mission team workers, some of whom they recognized from the photographs on the prayer notes that regularly arrived through their letter box at home.

Mum and Dad were soon involved in conversations with different people, and David was invited to be the one who sent an email to their grandad to confirm they'd arrived safely and to tell him a few details of the early days of their trip. Sitting down at the keyboard he thought for a few minutes about what he should say, before beginning to type. The thought of grandad made him feel slightly homesick for their lifestyle at home; it was so different here.

He finished typing and pressed 'Send' just as Uncle Richard announced that it was time to go. They headed out of the office and back down the street to the town centre, where it looked as if the contents of every shop had spilled out onto the pavements. David was amazed at the quantity and size of all the different metal cooking pots that gleamed brightly as the sun was reflected off them.

They stopped to watch a lady cooking what looked like huge doughnuts on a gas ring set on the ground. The barber across the street was cutting a man's hair without even looking at what he was doing because he was so interested in the onlookers.

'Here's a tip,' said Uncle Richard running his hand through his own hair: 'don't go to the barbers when there are visitors in town!'

Chapter ten:
HOSPITAL VISIT

Uncle Richard was keen that they visit the hospital to see the work he was involved in. David thought he was the only one who was unsure about going, until Emily said, 'I hope we don't see anything horrible.' Even Mum seemed a little anxious.

The journey to the hospital took about half an hour, and as they passed through a village, young children rushed to the roadside to wave at them.

The hospital buildings didn't look very different from the buildings they'd already seen in the town. They followed Uncle Richard across a courtyard to the front door, where they were greeted by a man wearing a white doctor's coat. He seemed very pleased to see them and was keen to show them around the hospital and introduce them to some of the patients.

A group of people looked up as they entered the nearest ward, and Uncle Richard was immediately surrounded by chattering, smiling men, women and children. He grasped their hands and patted the children on their heads as he tried to talk to as many people as he could. It was several minutes before David saw that many of them had hands that were terribly deformed.

'They're leprosy patients, David,' whispered Auntie Sophie, spotting the look of shock on his face.

'Leprosy?' he gasped, thinking of the Bible stories he'd heard in Sunday school, of how lepers were cast out of society. 'That's really contagious, isn't it?'

'No! You don't need to worry, you're not in any danger!' Auntie Sophie reassured him. 'It's very easily treated, but some of these poor people have just left it too late to come to the hospital, so their hands and sometimes their feet are badly affected and even have to be amputated. The problem is that they lose the feeling in their fingers and don't always realize, so they carry on cooking and sometimes burn themselves terribly without feeling any pain.'

'But if they get treated quickly, they'll be OK?' asked David, trying not to stare at a lady who had lost most of the fingers on one hand.

'If they come soon enough, they can be treated by a course of tablets. But they often feel ashamed or afraid that it's going to cost too much, and so they leave it until it's too late. And of course, once a person's lost their fingers, they can't be put back.'

They moved through to the next ward, where they met a man who was only able to stand upright because he was strapped to a frame.

'Come and meet Arshad,' said Uncle Richard. 'The poor guy fell out of a tree last year and broke his neck.'

Arshad was smiling and clearly enjoying being the centre of attention. David marvelled that he was in such good spirits when he was never going to be able to walk again. He resolved to stop moaning quite so much over trivial things as Uncle Richard spoke to the young man and interpreted his answers. Arshad was thankful to be alive and determined to learn a new trade so that he'd be able to earn his living again.

Arshad was fascinated to see that Dad had a camera and was almost overwhelmed when Dad let him look through the lens and even take a couple of photographs with it.

'Tell him that we'll get them printed off and then he can have them next time you come,' offered Dad, and David could tell from the man's face as he listened to Uncle Richard that he was very excited. He and Dad shook hands very enthusiastically as they parted.

'You've just made a young man very happy, John,' Uncle Richard said, smiling as they left the ward. 'That'll be the best thing that's happened to him in weeks.'

'You know, I nearly didn't bring the camera in case it looked as though I was being insensitive to people's injuries,' said Dad. 'I'm so glad I brought it; the look on Arshad's face is something I'll remember for ever.'

Uncle Richard patted him on the shoulder and led them into the kitchens next, where a lady was stirring a fragrant curry on a gas ring on the floor. David saw at once that her hands and feet were horribly misshapen. She smiled up at them as they watched, and, dipping the spoon into the curry, she offered it to Mum, who hesitated.

'She wants you to taste it, Margaret,' said Uncle Richard.

'Oh, I don't like to,' protested Mum; 'it seems wrong to take the food she's cooking for the patients.'

'No choice! You have to taste it!' repeated Uncle Richard. 'She'll be offended if you don't!'

So Mum knelt down on the floor and accepted the spoon. Her face lit up as she sipped the curry, and the lady smiled at her response.

'It's fantastic!' gasped Mum. 'Beautiful! Really beautiful! Thank you.' She handed back the spoon while Uncle Richard translated what she had said to the lady, who nodded and smiled broadly.

'Isn't she going to give us all a taste?' grumbled David as they left the kitchen.

'Absolutely not!' said Auntie Sophie laughing. 'She knows better than to offer it to teenagers with huge appetites! There'd be none left!'

'I hope you've enjoyed that,' said Uncle Richard as they left the hospital. 'I hope it's given you a better idea of what we're involved in here. There's a hospital shop over there, if you want to have a look inside. Most of what's on sale is made by the patients.'

David didn't bother going into the shop. He sat outside on a low wall while the rest of them did some shopping. Uncle Richard waited outside with him.

'What did you think? A bit shocking?'

'A bit, at first,' admitted David thoughtfully. 'Especially the people who had deformed hands and could have been treated. It makes you feel sad.'

'And angry!' exclaimed Uncle Richard. 'It makes me really mad! If only we could get into some of the rural villages and explain how easy it is to be treated! That's going to be my next project. Of course, it means I'll be away from home for maybe a week at a time, and that's tough on Auntie Sophie—and even more so on Rachel, because she won't understand.'

'It's quite hard even when you do understand,' mumbled David. 'We miss you so much at home, but now, seeing what you do in the hospital's made me realize what a fantastic job you're doing.'

He felt the colour rush into his cheeks; he hadn't expected to say anything so embarrassing.

'It means a lot to hear you say that, Dave,' said Uncle Richard. 'Oh my goodness! What has Rachel got on her head!'

David glanced up to see Dad and Mum coming out of the shop leading Rachel, who was wearing a bright yellow knitted hat. She stopped in front of the window to study her reflection. Uncle Richard laughed and went to join them, David following reluctantly. Trust Rachel to interrupt, just when he was having an important conversation with Uncle Richard! He scowled at her as she approached. But she didn't seem to notice; she just looked up at him and said, 'Hat!'

'If you think this is bad, wait till you see what Emily's buying!' warned Dad.

Chapter eleven:
IN THE MOUNTAINS

Emily squeezed into her seat at the breakfast table. 'I know they said we'd have to start off early, but this is ridiculous!' she moaned. 'I can't eat in the middle of the night!'

'You'll be very hungry later,' said Dad as he joined them; 'and I don't call half-past six the middle of the night!'

'I'm looking forward to this!' said David with a grin. 'It'll be something to tell the guys at school. Bet nobody else will have been climbing in the Himalayas!'

'Climbing?' echoed Mum as she entered the room. Everyone turned round to look at her. 'Are we going to be doing a big climb? Will I be able to make it?'

'We're not going up Everest!' said David as Mum pulled out a chair at the table; 'but we are in the most mountainous country in the world, so I think we can expect to climb a bit.'

'Mum!' gasped Emily, drawing everyone's attention away from David's rude remark; 'you're not wearing those trousers!'

'No, she's just taking them for a walk!' snorted David, adding more rudeness, and earning himself a stern look from Dad.

'What's wrong with them?' asked Mum lightly, smoothing down the creased flowery material. 'Auntie Sophie said I'd need to wear something comfortable for walking, so I am. It's not a fashion show! And I don't think we're likely to run into anybody we know!'

'It's certainly not a fashion show! Those haven't been fashionable for about fifty years! Just make sure you're not on any photographs!' said Emily, making everyone, including Mum, laugh.

'They're very comfy. And I'd be grateful if you'd keep your opinions about my wardrobe to yourself in future, Emily!' warned Mum.

'Technically, it's not the Himalayas,' said Uncle Richard as he placed a plate of toast in the middle of the table. 'As far as the locals are concerned, it's a bit of a hill!'

'Well, that's all right then,' said Mum with a nervous laugh; 'even I should be able to manage a bit of a hill!'

'It's probably best if you take a waterproof jacket or a thin fleece—it could be a bit chilly when we get to the top,' advised Auntie Sophie, 'especially if the mist comes down.'

The streets were already busy when they finally set out. Rachel was perched in a child carrier on Uncle Richard's back, drawing lots of attention as she waved a white handkerchief to passers-by. Now and again she draped it over Uncle Richard's face and laughed as he pretended to blow his nose on it.

It didn't take long for the road to start going uphill. David peeled off his fleece, tied it round his waist and marched ahead of the rest of the family to the next bend. He was accompanied by a small group of children with wide smiles and ragged clothes, who chattered and laughed and pointed at his rucksack. He lengthened his stride to try to escape them, but they were quick and nimble and soon caught up. When he reached the bend he stopped and waited for the rest of the family as the children chased each other, playing a game he didn't quite understand.

Uncle Richard was the first to catch up with him, even with Rachel on his back. As soon as Auntie Sophie arrived with Emily, she fished some sweets out of her rucksack and gave one to each of the children, who danced with delight and called out what David assumed were thanks, before stretching out their hands requesting more. Auntie Sophie shook her head and put the sweets back in her rucksack. David unwrapped his sweet and popped it quickly in his mouth, fearing that otherwise one of the children might look at him and he would feel obliged to give it away.

'These kids are driving me crazy,' grumbled David; 'they just won't leave me alone!'

'They'll turn back before long,' said Uncle Richard. 'Don't forget that they don't often see people like you. They find you fascinating, and as far as they're concerned, you're a millionaire!'

'Millionaire? Me?' laughed David. 'That's ridiculous! I'm always short of cash, and Emily won't lend me a penny!'

'If you've even got a penny,' said Uncle Richard, 'you're a millionaire compared with them.' He smiled and patted David on the back.

The sound of an engine straining up the hill reached their ears, and seconds later an old bus chugged into view; it was so overcrowded with people that David was amazed it could actually manoeuvre round the bend. Dozens of people were sitting on top of the bus; they waved as they went past, and the children suddenly found something else to amuse them, dancing off after the bus.

David took a sip from his water bottle as they prepared to set off again. 'You all right, Mum?'

Mum's face was very red and she looked exhausted already. 'Tell you what, David, as soon as we get home, I'm joining a keep-fit class! You go ahead. Don't wait for me!'

'Let's walk together,' said David; 'here, let me carry your bag.' He slung Mum's flimsy rucksack over his shoulder.

'Take your fleece off, Mum, then you won't be so hot.' She did as he said and he stuffed it into his own rucksack. 'Just say if you want it back.' He looked at her carefully; she didn't look as if she would be able to walk to the top of this bit, never mind over the hilltop.

Chapter twelve: MUM!

Once they rounded the bend, the road flattened out for a while and Mum found a reserve of energy from somewhere. Before long, she'd fallen into step alongside Auntie Sophie and Emily. David strode on until he was level with Dad and Uncle Richard. He listened to their conversation for a while and then sped up, leaving everyone behind, stopping only when the road forked and he was unsure which direction to take.

Even at this height there were people with weather-beaten faces sitting on their porches in front of little wooden houses. An old lady waved and smiled a toothless grin at David as he walked past. He put his hands together and said, '*Namaste*' before hurrying to sit on a rock and sip from his water bottle while he waited for the others.

Dad and Uncle Richard were the first to arrive. The sun was now blistering hot and they were both sweating.

'Let me take Rachel for a while,' said Dad, and carefully they transferred the child carrier in which Rachel was dozing from Uncle Richard's back to Dad's.

'That's kind of you to take Rachel,' gasped Auntie Sophie as she and Emily arrived. 'Let me just straighten her hat.'

She reached up and adjusted the bright yellow hat which had fallen over Rachel's eyes. 'Now where's your mum?'

Mum eventually appeared over the brow of the hill. She had no breath left to say anything, but accepted the bottle of water from David and swallowed a few mouthfuls.

An hour later, the path beneath their feet became narrow and very rocky, and a low mist obscured the view of the valley and the way ahead.

'Just keep together,' said Uncle Richard; 'you can't get lost, there's only one path to the top. We've not far to go now, and you'll be glad to know there's a tea shop right at the top.'

Clouds of mist swirled around them as they climbed steadily upwards. The temperature had now fallen by several degrees and David untied his fleece from around his waist and pulled it over his head. Mum gratefully accepted hers when she caught up, and she and David walked together the last few hundred metres up to the highest point of the hill.

'This is the best cup of tea I've ever tasted in my whole life!' said Mum as they sat in the café. 'I feel like a new woman!'

She laughed at all the jokes at her expense, though a cloud crossed her face when Uncle Richard announced that they should make a move and get through the forest in case it started to rain and it brought the leeches out.

'And watch out for snakes!' he called, swinging the child carrier back onto his shoulders. Rachel had enjoyed running around and grumbled slightly as she was strapped back into her seat.

'Count yourself lucky, Rachel!' said Mum. 'I wish someone would carry me! And I hope your daddy's joking about those snakes!'

A light breeze had blown the mist away, and just before they came down off the summit, Uncle Richard pointed out a pair of soaring birds below them. 'Eagles,' he said; 'just look at that wing span. Makes you realize what a wonderful thing God is promising us in the Bible when he says we'll soar on wings like eagles.'

'Isaiah chapter 40, I think,' added Dad, 'where he talks about running and not growing weary. Could be very useful that, Margaret!' he added with a wink at Mum.

'I'll settle for walking and not fainting!' muttered Mum.

The path downwards was steep and slippery, and when David found himself behind Emily, he couldn't resist tickling the back of her neck with a leaf he'd picked up. He was rewarded with a ringing scream.

'I thought it was a leech!' she yelled.

'Don't be silly!' teased David; 'that's a leech on your arm!' He grinned as she screamed again.

At last the ground beneath their feet levelled out and they joined a rocky pathway running alongside the river, where they stopped for a few minutes to sip from their water bottles.

They watched a harassed young boy trying to herd half a dozen scraggy goats along the path. He was almost weeping with frustration as one of the goats kept escaping from the herd, determined to go in the wrong direction. It scooted away towards the slope, where the grass was a bit greener. The boy now seemed to be in a dilemma: if he ran after the runaway goat, the rest of them would scatter.

'D'you think we should offer to help him, Uncle Richard?' asked David.

'You know anything about goats?' asked Uncle Richard.

David shook his head.

'Nor do I; we could make it worse. Better leave him to it,' advised Uncle Richard.

David watched with interest to see what the boy would do, but before the situation was resolved Uncle Richard was herding them back on to their path towards the town. The last view David had of the boy was of him skidding down the slope towards the runaway goat while the other goats scattered in all directions.

Finally, as the rooftops of the town came into sight they crossed a small stream into a gently sloping paddy field. Suddenly, Mum tripped up and fell into a shallow dyke.

'Oh no!' she cried, and everyone dashed to help her up. She waved away all their expressions of concern and offers of help and scrambled back onto her feet. 'I'm not hurt!' she said, 'but look at my trousers!' She pointed at a huge tear across her left knee. She tried, without success, to pull the edges together. 'Oh I don't believe it! They're ruined!'

'To be honest, Mum, I think they were ruined about ten years ago!' said Emily, and everyone laughed.

Chapter thirteen:
DAVID'S BIG DAY

David remembered it was his birthday as soon as he woke up. It was sure to be different than if they'd been at home but he was determined to make the best of it; besides, his parents had said that he could still go wall-climbing with some friends when they got back.

There was no sign of Emily and the house seemed very quiet. He glanced at his watch and saw that it was almost breakfast time; maybe everyone had overslept. He pulled on his clothes and wandered through to see if breakfast was ready.

As soon as he opened the door, a great chorus of 'HAPPY BIRTHDAY!' rang out. Nobody had overslept: they were all waiting for him! Mum kissed him, Auntie Sophie kissed him and Rachel kissed him, but he drew back as Emily approached.

'I'm not kissing you, even on your birthday!' she said laughing, and pushed a present into his arms. 'I know you won't be able to play with this till we get home, but I hope it's OK. You said you'd enjoyed playing it at Matt's house.'

David ripped off the paper to reveal an Xbox game that he knew he would love playing. 'Thanks, Em, that's great!'

Mum and Dad had bought him a new football shirt. 'Fantastic!' he yelled, holding it up against his chest; 'and

it's the new one for this season! I'm going to wear it now.'
He pulled his T-shirt over his head and slipped on the
new shirt. 'Oh, cool! Thank you so much! It's just what I
wanted!'

'There are a couple more things to open when we get
home,' explained Dad, handing over a card.

'And these are from us,' said Auntie Sophie, producing
some more parcels from under the table, which turned
out to be some football socks and a Nepalese game which
Uncle Richard said he'd explain after breakfast.

Rachel, having watched the proceedings, toddled over
with a handful of bricks from her toy box and dropped
them in his lap. She looked up at him expectantly.

'I think it's supposed to be a present,' murmured
Uncle Richard out of the corner of his mouth, and David
pretended to look at the bricks as though he'd never seen
them before, and thanked Rachel just as he had thanked
everyone else.

Before Rachel could present him with the entire
contents of the toy box, Uncle Richard scooped her up and
strapped her into her seat at the table so that breakfast
could begin.

'I thought we might hire some bikes this morning,'
suggested Uncle Richard after breakfast; 'there's a pretty
spectacular waterfall a few miles outside town. What do
you think? It's just for the four of us. I believe Auntie
Sophie and your mum have some important preparations
to make for tea. Somebody's birthday or something!'

David enjoyed the freedom of whizzing along on his
bike. Of course, it was nothing like the mountain bike
he had at home, but it was wonderful to feel the sun on

his face and the wind in his hair. The waterfall lived up to their expectations. Dad and Uncle Richard read the history of the falls on the tourist information boards, while he and Emily leaned over the railings as far as they dared, enjoying the feeling of the spray on their faces.

'Careful, guys!' shouted Uncle Richard. 'I just read about how a little girl drowned here when she fell over the railings! Your dad'll get very wet if he has to jump in after you!'

As they began to cycle back they could see the storm clouds moving in, threatening a return of the heavy monsoon rain. The first few spots of rain were falling as they reached the top of their street, and by the time they got to the front door the rain was pounding the footpaths and filling the drainage channels.

Chapter fourteen:
DISASTER!

The rain stopped shortly after lunch and Dad went with Uncle Richard to his office. David supposed he could have gone with them and emailed their grandad again, but he couldn't be bothered and he certainly didn't want to trail to the bazaar to see if the length of fabric that Mum had spotted was still there. He didn't mind staying behind; he would sit on the porch and read the instructions for the Xbox game.

He'd only been outside for two minutes when Auntie Sophie appeared in the doorway.

'David, would you mind if we leave Rachel with you?' she asked. 'She's fast asleep in the shade over there. I don't think she'll wake up. We'll be so much quicker if we don't have to wheel the buggy through the bazaar.'

David did mind; he was horrified at the thought of having to babysit, but he couldn't see how he could refuse. He wished he'd gone with the men now.

'There's nothing to it!' snapped Emily when Auntie Sophie went back inside the house to get her handbag. 'It's not exactly hard to look up every couple of minutes and check if she's still asleep. If she wakes up, give her a biscuit and come and find us in the bazaar. Looks like we're off—see you later.'

It's not exactly the perfect way to spend your birthday afternoon, thought David, losing interest in reading and spying the football on the porch. With Rachel soundly asleep, he saw no harm in opening the front gate and kicking the ball up and down the road, providing he checked on Rachel every couple of minutes.

He was so completely immersed in the joint pleasures of kicking the football again and wearing his new shirt that he never gave Rachel a thought until he heard her calling. Reluctantly, he went back into the garden and tried to jiggle the buggy about in the hope that she would go back to sleep. It took him less than a minute to realize that she was not going to sleep again, and he wondered what he should do. He didn't fancy joining the women in the bazaar, so he unfastened the straps so that Rachel could get out of the buggy. He was relieved when she immediately picked up her bucket and began to fill it with her plastic zoo animals.

'Dabey play,' she said, looking hopefully at him.

'I'm going to read,' he mumbled, and returned to his seat on the porch.

He didn't look up again until he heard the sound of the gate clattering back into its closed position. Fully expecting to see some of his family striding towards the porch, he was astonished to see that the pathway was empty. He spun round to look for Rachel, but the place where she'd been playing was also empty. He threw down his book and sprinted towards the gate, fumbled with the catch, failed to open it, then finally succeeded, yanked it open and raced out into the street.

Chapter fifteen:
LOSS AND LIES

There was no sign of Rachel. He ran into the middle of the road, looking first one way, then the other. The street was completely empty. He ran in the direction of the bazaar, looking in all the gardens he passed. Fully expecting to see Auntie Sophie and Mum turn the corner any second, he felt a huge wave of relief when they weren't anywhere to be seen.

'I just need more time,' he said to himself, before shouting loudly, 'Rachel! Where are you?'

The only sound was his own voice. He ran quickly to the other end of the street where it joined the main road to the lake. He shouted again and again, but there was no reply. His insides were churning with fear and guilt. He didn't know what to do for the best, and after running out onto the main road and frantically scanning each direction, only to find there was no sign of a tiny girl in a pink dress, he walked back down the street towards the house.

He had no idea what to do next. He couldn't ask anyone, and he didn't know where to begin looking. He resolved to look inside the house. If she wasn't there, he would have to go to the bazaar.

He shouted her name again as he approached the front of the house, and suddenly he heard the sound of a child crying. Running towards the source of the noise, he saw that Rachel had fallen into the water-filled drainage channel. She cried even harder when she saw him and held up her arms. He reached down and lifted her out of the gulley; she was wet and dirty, and she'd grazed her knees and elbows.

'Oh Rachel, I'm so sorry. Don't cry,' pleaded David as he carried her back into the garden and locked the gate.

He had no idea what he was supposed to do, but it made sense to get Rachel cleaned up and to change her clothes. He would think of an excuse as to how the incident had happened; thankfully Rachel wasn't old enough to tell them the truth.

It was a shame that Maiya didn't work in the afternoons because she would have washed the dirty dress for him. In the end he did it himself, after he'd washed Rachel's arms and legs and put her into the first clean things he could see in her bedroom. He was just pegging out the dress when Dad and Uncle Richard returned. They listened to his tale of a fall in the garden where there was a muddy puddle, and even though he caught Uncle Richard looking at him curiously as he gave all the details, he was pretty sure that he'd got away with it. Rachel was none the worse, and when the women returned he told them the same tale and was heralded as a bit of a hands-on hero for sorting it all out.

The birthday tea, complete with a delicious chocolate cake, took David's mind off what had happened and the lies he'd told to cover up his carelessness. Just as the sun was setting Uncle Richard went out into the garden to bring in Rachel's toys. At last they heard him washing his hands in the kitchen sink.

'Funny thing,' he said, settling himself into the cane chair nearest the window, 'I couldn't find Rachel's bucket, which is where she keeps the zoo animals. Do you know where it was? Out in the street, down the gulley! I only spotted it because the gulley was overflowing; the bucket was wedged over the drain so the water wasn't draining properly. Weird.'

That night, David lay in bed thinking through the day's events. It was great to get such nice presents, especially the football shirt. He really hadn't expected so many gifts, or for them to make it such a special day, but the incident with Rachel rested heavily on his mind. He knew they'd been very lucky; she could have really hurt herself when she fell into the gulley. She could even have drowned. He pushed that thought away as quickly as it had entered his mind, but he knew it was true. And he had told so many lies and half-truths, and he had a horrible, horrible feeling that Uncle Richard knew or at least suspected that it hadn't happened as he said.

Somewhere in the room the little gecko was creeping around—he hoped it wouldn't come anywhere near him while he was asleep. He pummelled his pillow and buried his face in it. He felt terrible; it had certainly been a birthday to remember—but not for very good reasons.

Chapter sixteen:
A Trip to Church

'Church?!' spluttered David as his head appeared through the T-shirt he was pulling on. 'We're going to church? In Nepal?'

'We talked about it last night,' said Mum in a tone of voice that he recognized; there would be no point in arguing: she would never give way.

'Nobody said anything to me,' he muttered.

'It would probably be more accurate to say that nobody said anything you could hear when you had your headphones stuck in your ears listening to whatever you were listening to!' said Mum. 'We talked about it last night when we sat down after dinner, after we'd washed up.'

'I didn't think we'd be going to church in Nepal!' said David stubbornly.

'Why on earth not?' asked Mum. 'You surely didn't think Uncle Richard and Auntie Sophie stopped going to church when they got here. Did you?'

The truth was that David had never given it so much as a thought, but as Mum was in full flow he didn't have to say anything.

'They need fellowship,' she continued, 'and friends. And God can still speak to people in Nepal, you know, just as much as He speaks to people back home in our church.'

'So how come He never says anything to me?' mumbled David under his breath after Mum left the room.

'Probably 'cos you're never listening,' teased Emily, entering the room with a pile of ironing that Maiya had done.

'I didn't know we were going to church,' said David.

'I could probably write a thousand books about what you don't know,' Emily said giggling, and dropping the pile of clothes onto one of the beds, she darted out of the room as David hurled his sandal at her.

He was still muttering under his breath when they left the house an hour later. 'I thought we were going to the lakeside today.'

'Well, you thought wrong, didn't you! That's tomorrow,' said Emily, taking Rachel by the hand. 'Uncle Richard says this is Rachel's favourite event of the week,' she added.

'Yeah, it would be,' whispered David, kicking a stone across the road; 'and also it's Saturday, not Sunday!'

Things got even worse for him when they arrived at church. Uncle Richard turned to them and said, 'Oh, by the way, they'll invite you to stand up and introduce yourselves and greet the congregation. Best if I nudge you, John, when it's the right time, then everyone can copy you. Just stand up, say "*Namaste*" and something like, "I'm John and I'm from England." OK?'

Dad was nodding, but David thought, 'No, it's not OK! I don't want to do that!' The day had just got even worse, but no one else complained so he kept his mouth shut.

The inside of the church building was nothing like his church at home. There were no seats apart from a few benches along the back wall. Lots of people had already gathered and were sitting cross-legged on the floor, the men and boys on one side and the women and girls on the other. There was no hum of noise and chatter as there was in his church; people sat almost in silence, some with their heads bowed and some with their eyes closed. An elderly lady approached them, took Mum by the arm and indicated that she should sit on one of the benches. Uncle Richard laughed and whispered to Mum, 'She must think you're very old!'

'I don't care,' Mum whispered back, 'as long as I don't have to sit on the floor for a couple of hours!' The ladies shuffled up to make room for her and she beamed happily at them.

'Couple of hours?' echoed David as he followed Uncle Richard into a space where they sat cross-legged on the floor. Across the room, Emily sat down next to Auntie Sophie, and Rachel pottered up and down, smiling at different people.

Eventually a man stood up at the front, said what David presumed were words of welcome, and then picked up a guitar and began to strum.

Chapter seventeen:
DAVID IS BORED

It was boring. There was no doubt about that. It was nearly as bad as looking at Auntie Pat's photos of her frequent trips to some uninteresting place in the middle of nowhere in the middle of Africa, only it went on longer! David had dreaded having to stand up and introduce himself, but that was nothing compared with the overwhelming dullness of the service. He was also sharing a Bible with a young man who didn't seem to understand that he couldn't read a word of Nepalese and had no idea whether they were in the Old or New Testament, never mind which book.

Lots of people contributed to the proceedings, and now and again they all stood up to sing. Some of the tunes were familiar, and Dad joined in enthusiastically, singing along in English. Eventually a man stood at the lectern and began to speak. David presumed this was the sermon, and although he had no expectations that it would be short, he truly hoped that it would be the last item on the order of service. The young man next to him had given up trying to share his Bible and was studying it carefully as he listened intently to the speaker. David looked at the writing on the open pages; the letters were so alien to him that he couldn't even begin to guess what the sermon was about.

The sunlight was filtering in through half-open shutters and making strange shapes on the wall as it highlighted different sections of the uneven plaster. There was a small fuzzy blob behind the speaker's head, and the more David looked at it, the more it looked like a long-legged sheep. To the left and a bit higher up the wall, another fuzzy mess took on the shape of a herd of sheep, and it reminded David of the parable of the lost sheep. The lone, long-legged sheep appeared to have drifted away from the herd, and he wondered if the light would play enough tricks on his eyesight to return it to the sheepfold. He thought about the goats they'd seen on their walk, and wondered whether the boy had managed to capture the runaway.

Slowly, slowly, the light moved across the wall, and still the preacher preached. David glanced across to where the women were sitting. Rachel was sitting on Auntie Sophie's knee and, although David couldn't see her face, he guessed from the complete lack of movement that she was asleep. He wished he could sleep too. The sheep on the wall had now merged into one big mass and it looked as though the herd had been reunited.

David's thoughts turned to his church at home and the youth group of which he was a member. It was sometimes very hard to feel a part of the group; sometimes it seemed as if everyone but him was getting a special message directly from God and he was the only one struggling to make sense of his faith. It wasn't that he didn't believe; it was just that he didn't feel as if he had any personal relationship with God. Other people talked about how God had said this or that to them through a passage in the Bible or through what the preacher had said, but it didn't feel real to David.

He went to church because he had to, and although he enjoyed the youth group, none of his friends had any idea what it was like to have half your family living on the other side of the world serving God on the mission field. He was beginning to feel as if he didn't fit in anywhere. Recently, even some of the cool guys, like Matt and Luke, had made decisions to follow Jesus. He glanced again at the wall, which was now fully lit. The sheep were all in the fold, and he really wished he was one of them. 'God, I don't know if it's you that has made Matt and Luke so different recently,' he prayed in the quietness of his own thoughts, 'but if it is, then that's what I want too.'

All around him, people were now starting to move. Dad and Uncle Richard were standing up and stretching their aching legs, so David leapt to his feet, confident that the service was finally at an end. A couple more songs and it was over, and they were heading for the doorway.

Lots of people shook their hands as they went out. David nodded and smiled and said '*Namaste*' about a hundred times as they filed out onto the sunlit street.

Chapter eighteen:
EXPLANATION

'I thought we'd go out for lunch,' said Uncle Richard as he led them away from the church. 'There's a really nice restaurant we sometimes go to after church. It's very child-friendly and the meatballs are fantastic. Everyone in favour, walk this way.'

He swung Rachel up onto his shoulders and led the way through a maze of streets to a smart-looking building with a veranda where people were eating and drinking. Within no time they were sitting at a long table on that same veranda sipping ice-cold juice through straws and waiting for the arrival of the famous meatballs.

'What did you think of our church?' asked Uncle Richard.

'Interesting experience,' said Dad. 'I wasn't sure I'd ever get the feeling back in my legs, though!'

'Well, those benches were a bit hard!' said Mum with a laugh.

'Can you understand enough of the language to be able to follow what's going on?' asked Emily.

'Sometimes it's harder than others,' confirmed Auntie Sophie. 'Today wasn't so bad—he was talking about the lost sheep.'

David turned to look at his aunt so quickly, he felt everyone must have noticed.

'What about the lost sheep?' he asked.

'Well, about how we can feel on the outside of the flock, and how easy it is to wander away,' explained Auntie Sophie. 'He went on to talk about the lost son as well, and how there's always a way back to God if we want to find it. God is always searching for us.'

The meatballs arrived, and much praise was heaped on their appearance and then their taste. David ate in silence. He couldn't believe that the sermon had covered exactly what he'd been thinking about, and he wondered if this was what it was like to experience God speaking to you. He hardly noticed as the plates were cleared away and replaced with dishes of frozen yoghurt desserts.

'You're very quiet, Dave,' said Uncle Richard eventually. 'Are you OK?'

'Fine,' replied David rather abruptly; 'just thinking.'

'Well, I'll tell you what I'm thinking,' said Auntie Sophie with a smile. 'Apart from wondering how Rachel's got more tomato sauce down her dress than in her tummy, I'm thinking that we'd better make a move. The rain's coming. Look at the sky over there! We'll be lucky if we can get back before it starts pouring down. Better ask for the bill, Richard.'

By the time Dad and Uncle Richard had decided who was going to pay the bill, the sky had become leaden with thick, heavy clouds, and they could hear the thunder rumbling.

'We should've brought umbrellas!' yelled Uncle Richard. 'Run! It's every man for himself!'

He picked up Rachel and started to run. 'Can you hear the rain in the distance? It's coming this way!' he yelled over his shoulder, and sure enough, David could soon hear the sound of heavy rain hammering down as it approached. He raced past Mum and Auntie Sophie, who had fished out an umbrella from the depths of one of their bags and were walking arm-in-arm, trying to include Emily in the tiny space where it was dry.

The rain caught up with them at the top of the street where they lived. The drains and water channels were overflowing within seconds. David had never in all his life seen anything like this rain that flooded the road and filled their sandals.

Chapter nineteen:
THE ROAD TO BENI

'It's not that long since they built this road,' said Uncle Richard, as the Land Rover, with Dipendra once more at the wheel, clattered and bumped along the dirt track. 'In the old days, you had to walk everywhere! When we first came to Nepal, we lived in a place called Bungadoven. It was a tiny village right up in the mountains, miles from anywhere. You couldn't get there by road—you just went as far as you could in the Land Rover and then you had to walk the rest of the way.'

'How long did that take?' asked Mum, looking horrified.

'Two or three days, depending on the weather,' said Uncle Richard. 'Tell you what: we didn't go back to Pokhara very often. In fact, we didn't go anywhere!'

'How awful!' said Mum.

'What about all your stuff?' asked Emily.

'We had a team of men to carry everything for us,' explained Uncle Richard.

'Bit like going up Everest with your own Sherpas!' joked David. 'Emily would've needed a team of men just to carry her stuff. Her case was overweight!'

'It was not!' argued Emily. 'And anyway, I had heaps of stuff in my case that didn't belong to me.'

'Tell you what, though,' said Auntie Sophie, 'some of that journey actually felt like going up Everest—it was exhausting! Sometimes God's call is very hard to follow; Bungadoven was tough. We had a lady who came in to work for us most days. On the days she didn't come we could never get the stove to light, so we were freezing cold and couldn't make anything hot to eat!'

'And that happened every time she had a day off?' asked Dad.

'Most times, though we'd just about got the hang of it about a fortnight before our placement finished!'

'And what about when that leopard ate next door's dog?' said Uncle Richard.

'Yeah, that was a bit scary, especially when the toilet was just a hole outside! And do you remember when that man moved into the shed at the end of our garden? It was quite tricky getting him to leave!' added Auntie Sophie with a laugh. 'On the whole, I've got to say that living in Pokhara is a lot easier.'

'So this journey is absolute luxury,' said Uncle Richard. The Land Rover jolted over a big pothole that rattled their bones as he spoke.

David peered out of the window. 'We're really close to the edge!' he announced cheerfully. 'And then there's a sheer drop! What if we meet something coming the other way?' he asked, winding the window down.

'Be a bit of a squeeze,' said Uncle Richard; 'and it will involve a bit of reversing and quite a lot of falling out over who has the right of way!'

'How many times do cars fall over the side?' asked David, leaning out of the window as far as he could.

'We try not to think about that!' confessed Uncle Richard.

'Whoa! It's a long way down!' said David. 'Aren't you scared, Mum?'

'No,' murmured Mum, though she had her eyes tightly closed.

No one spoke very much while the road was so narrow, but eventually David became aware that they were going downhill, and a few miles further on they saw a long bridge suspended across the widest river David had ever seen.

'WOW! Look at that bridge!' shouted Emily. 'Is it made out of ropes? Is it safe? Is it strong enough to walk across?'

'So many questions! Some of the older bridges are made out of rope, but this one is made of steel wires. It's still a bit wobbly, though, especially when there are lots of people on it.'

'It looks amazing!' said Emily. 'Have you ever been across it, Auntie Sophie?'

Auntie Sophie laughed again. 'Hundreds of times, Emily, and in a few minutes you'll be going across it! It's the only way into Beni. There are no cars there; Dipendra will park here on this side of the river and we'll meet him tomorrow.'

Chapter twenty:
MORE TALKING!

David waited his turn to step onto the bridge. He'd let everyone else go ahead of him as he wanted to drink in this new experience without anyone in his family urging him to hurry up. He closed his eyes for a second and imagined himself in one of the adventure films he loved so much. He pictured himself diving across the bridge as his enemies closed in behind him, hacking with massive swords at the ropes until he was left dangling on the end of one rope over a surging torrent of water. He was just imagining the mighty swing he would have to take to save himself, and the beautiful heroine he'd already rescued from the cave where she was imprisoned, when someone gave him a hard shove in the back. Jolted back to reality, he turned round and was astonished to see a man leading a mule train onto the bridge. He couldn't tell what the man was shouting but he knew that it was a command to get moving or get out of the way.

He raced across the bridge, pursued by the mules with their jingling harnesses, and joined the rest of his family as they gazed around, taking in their new surroundings.

'Poor things,' said Emily when she saw the size of the panniers the mules were carrying.

'They're bringing the stock in for the shops, Emily. Without the mules the town would grind to a halt,' explained Uncle Richard; 'and here come the building materials!' They watched as another man drove a single mule carrying long steel poles past them.

'If they didn't use the mules, the people would have to carry the stuff into town, and it would probably be the women doing it,' said Uncle Richard as he led them down a street to the centre of the town.

Emily was still talking about the mules carrying such heavy weights when they arrived in front of a gaudy building set in a lush, colourful garden. A sign above the front door announced that they had arrived at their destination: 'The Silver Mountain Hotel'.

The lady who owned the hotel was expecting them and rushed out to greet them warmly: 'Come, come, follow me. Best hotel in town, I can promise you—clean beds, good food, and a Western toilet for you, Madam.' She took Mum by the wrist and led her up the steps and into the shade of the hotel hallway. Mum beamed at everyone and allowed herself to be led up the stairs to view the best room in Beni.

David and Emily's room contained two beds and nothing else. They dumped their rucksacks on the beds and, having discovered that Uncle Richard and Auntie Sophie's room was equally basic, they went in search of Mum and Dad's room with its famous Western toilet.

With only a one-night stop in Beni, Auntie Sophie was keen to take them around the town, to introduce them to the friends they had made when they worked there, and to show them the house where they had lived when they first had Rachel.

'It's like a medieval town,' whispered David to Emily as they walked down the main street. The road was just a dirt track, and many of the houses and shops had shutters over their windows but no glass.

'Watch what you're stepping on!' called Dad. 'Don't forget, the mules came down here a few minutes ago!'

A group of men sitting on the street corner outside a coffee house watched them as they passed. Uncle Richard called out a greeting and the men nodded at them suspiciously.

'There's the cinema!' cried Auntie Sophie. 'That brings back memories of trying to get Rachel to sleep while the outdoor speakers broadcast the soundtrack of the film at a million decibels! And here's where we lived.'

They stood in front of a small house with shuttered windows. 'I don't know the people who live here now,' said Auntie Sophie, 'or we could have asked if we could show you round. It's a bit like our house in Pokhara, but smaller.'

'Except there's no glass in the windows!' observed David.

'Yeah, it was very chilly in the winter,' confirmed Uncle Richard.

It seemed as though the whole town had turned out to look at them; wherever they went they were followed by people who stood unashamedly listening in to their conversations. One or two old friends turned up to greet Uncle Richard and Auntie Sophie and exclaim at how much Rachel had grown.

They were invited into the home of one of Uncle Richard's colleagues and climbed up the steep stairway to his third-floor living room, passing a small bathroom on the first floor and a kitchen, half of which was open to the elements, on the second floor.

Ramesh welcomed them warmly into his home and invited them to take a seat, before encouraging his wife to bring drinks for everyone. She nodded her head and left the room. They could hear her feet tapping down the stairs.

As David and Emily sat next to the open window, the sounds and smells of the street drifted up to them.

'Look at that little boy!' whispered Emily, nudging David. 'Look at the mask he's wearing. It's just a bit of old card with eyeholes torn into it.'

David watched the boy chasing a group of his friends. As soon as he touched one of them, he ripped off the mask and handed it over and the chase began again.

'Looks like they're having fun,' murmured David, and he wished he was down there with them instead of shut up in this stifling room, waiting for yet another cup of tea.

'Makes you realize you don't really need all the stuff we've got to have fun, doesn't it?' said Emily.

'Does it?' David looked at his sister in surprise. He thought about his birthday gifts, and he was pretty sure he'd enjoy his Xbox game a lot more than running round in a paper mask.

'Just listen to them laughing!' Emily said smiling.

Suddenly aware of the clinking of cups, David turned round to see what was happening in the room. Ramesh's wife was holding a tray in front of him. She smiled and nodded, and he took one of the cups she offered. She watched him closely until he had taken a sip, and then, satisfied that he was pleased, she moved on to offer her tray to the ladies.

Then the talking began. Life seemed to be all about talking, thought David—and drinking tea.

Chapter twenty-one:
BAD MOOD

The sunlight streaming through the thin curtains awoke David the next morning. If he was honest, he knew was in a bad mood even before he got out of bed and looked out of the window across the rooftops to where the town was already bustling with life. This morning, the noise of people clearing their throats and spitting in the gutters, the call of the vegetable sellers and the sound of children shrieking and laughing were all deeply irritating. Somewhere not far away a cockerel was cock-a-doodle-doo-ing for all he was worth.

The puddles left by the heavy overnight rain were already steaming as the temperatures rose. It was going to be another hot, sticky day.

Another day, thought David—another day of sweating and wandering around meeting people he wasn't interested in and eating stuff that he didn't like or didn't want to try. What wouldn't he give for a burger or some chips! He wondered what his friends were doing on their holidays. He was pretty sure they would be having more fun than he was having.

He fished his towel out of his rucksack and went down the landing to his parents' room. Dad was in the shower when he got there and, although Mum said he could stay and wait, he sighed and went back to his own room.

'What's up with you?' asked Emily, raising herself up on one elbow in her bed as he chucked his towel into the corner.

'Nothing,' he replied, 'unless you count being in a place that's doing my head in.'

Emily looked shocked. 'What do you mean?'

'There's nothing to do,' moaned David. 'All we do is visit people and drink tea. Horrible tea.'

'What did you expect?' said Emily sharply. 'We're on the other side of the world, in a poor country, in a hill community. Some of these people have never even left the town. Why can't you just enjoy the experience? It's not for long—we're going back to Pokhara this afternoon.'

'Like that's where it's all happening!' David muttered.

'You're unbelievable!' snapped Emily. 'We're getting the chance to see what Uncle Richard and Auntie Sophie did when they lived out here, and to just *be* with them. You were the one who was so desperate to see them. It's a brilliant experience, something we'll remember for ever. And they appreciate us being here so much—it's a real bonding time for our family.'

'All right, all right, get off your soapbox!' David snapped back. 'It's just me, then, who's fed up with everything revolving around what Rachel's doing.'

Emily jumped out of bed. 'What's it got to do with Rachel?' she shouted. 'That's selfish and mean, David, and it's also not true! She has to do what we're doing, and I don't hear her grumbling when I bet she'd rather be at home playing with her toys!'

She snatched up her towel, stormed out of the room and slammed the door.

'Hey! I was going first!' David dropped onto the bed and punched the pillow. He knew she was right, and that made him madder than ever.

He was still in a mood when they went down to breakfast. Emily glared at him across the table, and Mum caught the look that passed between them.

'What's wrong with you two?' she whispered.

'Nothing,' said David.

'Him,' said Emily.

Mum looked at David.

'I don't know. Nothing. Missing home a bit, that's all,' David said, coming up with the first excuse that came into his mind.

Emily tutted. But Mum smiled at him. 'Of course you are. You're bound to be. Everything's so different. Just try to enjoy every experience. Now, eat up— this morning we're going to visit a family with a little boy who's the same age as Rachel.'

'Great!' said David. He glared at Emily and mouthed 'shut up' at her before looking down at his plate and eating whatever was on it.

Chapter twenty-two:
LEFT BEHIND

The trek through the town was just the same as the day before, side-stepping puddles and animal dung, dodging rain showers and seeing the same people sitting on the same street corners in exactly the same places and positions they'd been in yesterday. David wouldn't have minded betting that they were having exactly the same conversations.

Dad noticed it as well; he said, 'Life moves very slowly here, doesn't it?'

'You can say that again!' confirmed Uncle Richard. 'That bloke in the white shirt's probably been sitting there for the last five years—he was there when we lived here! It's a very different way of life here. Time doesn't mean the same here as it does at home, where we're all rushing round to meet our schedules. We've got a lot to learn from these people.'

'Here we are!' said Auntie Sophie cheerfully. 'This is where Ashmi lives. She's such a lovely lady and worked very hard for us when we lived here. She has a little boy called Ashok who's the same age as Rachel.'

The front door was wide open, revealing one neat room with a bed in the corner. The shelves were full of highly polished metal dishes. Ashmi came to greet them and seemed overawed to have so many people visiting her. She was holding the hand of a very frail-looking little boy. She let him go long enough to clasp her hands in front of her, bow and whisper, 'Namaste'; the little boy copied her.

Auntie Sophie gave her a bag containing a gift. The lady nodded and looked pleased, though she kept looking anxiously at all the guests.

'I think we've overwhelmed her,' muttered Uncle Richard to Dad. 'It's probably best if you and I wander off for a while.'

He turned to Auntie Sophie. 'John and I will come back in about half an hour, Soph. We'll go and have a look at the building site down by the river.'

David opened his mouth to protest; he didn't want to stay if the men were going, but nobody took any notice of him, and he and Emily were ushered into the small garden at the side of the house along with Mum, Auntie Sophie and the children.

'Great!' he muttered to Emily.

'You should have said you wanted to go with them,' she whispered back.

'Well, it's too late now, isn't it?' he said angrily. 'Not that anybody's bothered what I want to do!' He glanced at his watch.

Once the men had gone, Ashmi was more relaxed, and hurried back into the house to make some drinks.

'Oh dear,' whispered Mum, 'I do hope she's not going to give us what she would be using for their dinner.'

'She'd be mortified if she couldn't give us refreshments,' Auntie Sophie whispered back; 'but don't worry, I brought her lots of things.'

Rachel and Ashok were eyeing each other cautiously. Rachel held out the doll she was carrying, and Ashok studied it, then stretched out a tentative finger and touched the doll's black hair. Within minutes the toddlers were playing happily together.

Half an hour dragged by. Ashmi served them all tea and answered all the questions Auntie Sophie was asking her. David had no idea what they were saying, and as Mum and Emily seemed intent on excluding him from their conversation, he withdrew into a sulky silence.

It didn't take long for Rachel and Ashok to become the best of friends. The doll had been abandoned and they were huddled together side by side sifting soil through their hands.

Out in the roadway a group of little boys were kicking a punctured football between them, and as it didn't bounce, much of their game consisted of one or other of them retrieving the ball from wherever it had landed.

'Go and play with them if you like,' suggested Mum.

David shook his head. 'No point,' he said; 'it's not even a proper ball.'

Mum was drawn into the conversation between Auntie Sophie and Ashmi, and David noticed that, even though she didn't understand a word, she looked interested and smiled a lot.

Emily had gone to play with Rachel and Ashok. David stared up the road, willing Dad and Uncle Richard to return. Eventually, they came into view and he heaved a sigh of relief. He looked at his watch again; it was unbelievable how slowly the time crawled by in this place.

Three o'clock couldn't come fast enough; he was longing to cross that bridge again and get back to the Land Rover.

Chapter twenty-three:
MISSING!

'You look as if you didn't enjoy your time with the ladies, Dave,' said Uncle Richard as they walked away from Ashmi's house.

'It was a bit boring,' admitted David, 'especially when I couldn't tell what they were saying.'

'You know, we should have invited you to come with me and your dad and have a look at what they're building down the road. Bit thoughtless of us—sorry about that. We were a bit too keen to get away ourselves!'

'Doesn't matter,' said David, not altogether truthfully.

They walked very slowly so that Rachel could keep up with them. Now and again someone carried her for a while, but mostly she ran between them, taking first one hand and then another.

'Look who's here!' exclaimed Auntie Sophie as they turned a corner and saw a young man approaching them. As David was sighing at the prospect of another cup of tea, he felt Rachel slip her tiny hand into his. He looked down at her. She smiled and said, 'Hello, Dabey! Carry?'

'No,' said David crossly, shaking his hand free. 'Ask Emily.'

A frown creased Rachel's face and she held up her arms. 'No, Dabey!'

David heaved a huge sigh. 'I said no, Rachel! Go to Emily; I'm too hot.'

A sudden thud on his leg made him spin round. The little gang of footballers had kicked their ball at him.

'Oi! Watch out!' he shouted, kicking the ball back to them. In two seconds it was kicked back to him again, and before he knew it he was involved in the game they were playing. He forgot about being hot and fed up and found new energy to kick the ball backwards and forwards to them.

They played for at least ten minutes until the young man said goodbye to the adults and went on his way.

'Nice guy, Rajesh; I enjoyed working with him,' said Uncle Richard. 'Now let's go and get some lunch at The Silver Mountain, then we can get our stuff together and go and meet Dipendra. Want to ride on Daddy's shoulders back to the hotel, Rachel?'

He looked around. 'Where's Rachel?' There was panic in his voice. They all looked at one another frantically.

'RACHEL?!' shouted Uncle Richard.

'OK, now keep calm,' said Dad, as Auntie Sophie began to cry. 'She can't have gone far. Who saw her last? Was she here when we met Rajesh?'

Everyone was shaking their heads as a cold hand of fear and shame gripped David's insides. Surely he hadn't been the last one to see her when he shook her little hand away?

'She was with you, David, wasn't she, when we saw Rajesh,' said Auntie Sophie in a shaky voice. 'I was going to introduce him to her, but I thought she'd gone with you to play football with those boys.'

David could barely look at her. 'She didn't come with me. I thought she was with ...' He stopped; he had been going to lay the blame on Emily. 'I'm sorry,' he said, and tears came to his own eyes. 'I thought she was safe with all of you. I never ...'

Mum put her arm around him. 'It's all right, no one's blaming you. It's not your fault. We'll soon find her. She can't have gone far.'

Dad took control of the search. 'Right! Now try to keep calm, everyone. Richard, you retrace our steps on that side of the street. Sophie, you take that side. Go in every shop and every house where there's an open door. Emily and David, stay right here—she might come back here. Mum and I will go down ... er ... this way.' He pointed towards the river but didn't say the word. 'And pray! OK?'

David turned to Emily as the others left to search. 'Please don't say anything, Em. It's my fault, I know it is, and I feel terrible.'

Emily touched his arm gently. 'Nobody's blaming you, Dave. They'll find her. Little children are always wandering off.'

'I pushed her away when she wanted me to pick her up,' said David.

'It's not your fault—you were hot and tired. Small children can be really hard work. She'll be OK.'

'What if ...?' He stopped because no words could express the horror of them not finding her.

'Just pray,' said Emily kindly, 'with your eyes open, though.'

David struggled to pray anything except 'O Lord, please forgive me, and please bring Rachel back safely.'

'I'm going to look down some of the streets,' David said suddenly. 'I can't just stand here!'

Emily began to pick up the bags, but he stopped her. 'No, Em! You've got to stay here in case she comes back. Wait for the others.'

'Don't you get lost as well,' she called after him as he raced between the buildings towards Ashmi's house. There were so many places a small child could hide without being seen. He looked behind every bin and in every doorway, calling her name repeatedly, but there was no sign of her and no answering call.

Ashmi was in her garden and looked up and recognized David. He thought she was going to go back inside her house, but she only disappeared for a moment and returned with Ashok.

'Rachel!' he gasped as he reached her. 'Have you seen Rachel?'

The smile disappeared from her face. 'Rachel?' she repeated slowly, shaking her head, and he knew that she hadn't seen Rachel since their visit earlier.

'O God, help me to find her,' he prayed. 'Show me where she is, PLEASE!'

Realizing that he had spoken aloud and that people were looking at him, he sprinted back the way he'd come, emerging from the side street next to the cinema. He could see Emily in the distance, still standing alone in the middle of the road, and he made his way slowly towards her, looking in all the doorways he passed.

Emily called to him as he approached. 'Nothing?'

He shook his head. 'No. I thought she might have wandered back to Ashmi's house, but she's not there. Are the others back yet?'

'I thought she might have made her way back to The Silver Mountain,' said Emily. 'Auntie Sophie's gone to see. Uncle Richard's gone down that street there.' She pointed to an alleyway between the shops.

David put his hands over his eyes, then threw his head back and looked up into the sky, dragging his hands through his hair.

'I'll go down this side of the street!' he bellowed.

'Dave!' shouted Emily. 'They've already looked ...!'

But David ignored her and set off at full pelt, running into each shop, yelling Rachel's name loudly.

He turned back when he reached the top of the street. It was hopeless. He had no idea where to look next.

The only thing he was sure about was that it was his fault. He thought about Rachel blowing kisses at him in church.

He remembered that he'd been thinking about the shepherd rescuing the lost sheep while, unknown to him, the preacher had been speaking on the subject of the Good Shepherd.

'God, help me to find her!' he prayed again.

'No sign of her,' he said to Emily when he reached her. 'What if somebody's taken her?'

'I don't think that's likely!' whispered Emily.

Suddenly, he saw a tiny flash of red moving unsteadily along the balcony of the building across the road.

'She's there!' he yelled. 'I think she's up there!'

Emily looked in the direction he was pointing.

'Oh no!' screamed Emily. 'The balcony railings are broken at that end—if she gets there, she'll fall!'

'Don't shout her name, Em, just stay here in case they come back ... AND PRAY!' bellowed David desperately, and he sprinted across the road, looking for the stairway that led up the side of the building.

Chapter twenty-four: RESCUE!

The first stairway David tried led to a closed door, but from the top of the steps he could see the flight of steps that led to the balcony where Rachel was. He leapt down his staircase and on to the one in the next building, sprinting up the steps two at a time. He nodded at an old lady who was sitting in a doorway, confused by his sudden arrival. By the time he reached the balcony, he could barely breathe. And there Rachel was, toddling towards the broken railings!

'RACHEL!' he yelled.

She stopped, turned round, smiled, waved, and almost lost her balance as she called back, 'Hello, Dabey!'

David held out his arms. 'Come on, back this way, Rachel,' he gasped. She laughed and turned away, expecting him to chase her. He called her name again. 'Rachel! Don't go that way—come to me. Come and see what I've got in my pocket!'

As soon as she looked at him, he pretended to get something out of his pocket and peep through his fingers at it.

'Are you coming? Come and see what I've found.'

She started to run towards him, but then she dropped the doll she was carrying.

She stopped.

She turned.

The doll rolled over, once, twice, three times, slipping away down the sloping decking towards the broken railings.

Rachel let out a cry of indignation and began to follow it.

With horror, David saw her speed up, struggling to keep her balance on the uneven surface. She was going to fall through the broken railings down onto the roadway below. A loud creaking sound sent a shiver of fear down his spine as he realized that the decking was beginning to break away from the structure of the house.

If he had had longer to decide he probably would have been more cautious, but there was no time: his tiny cousin was toddling towards disaster! He bounded down the balcony, fearing that every footstep would break the fragile balcony and send them both plunging to their deaths.

'O God,' he prayed, 'please help me to save her!'

He grabbed Rachel just inches from the edge of the balcony. The black-haired doll plummeted through the railings and down onto the street. With Rachel tightly clutched against his chest, David inched his way back along the balcony, trying to keep his feet against the house wall. She wriggled and cried and tried to push him away, stretching out her little arms to where her doll had fallen.

He reached the corner of the house and the safety of the stairway at the exact moment Uncle Richard bounded up onto the top step. The terror on his face was quickly replaced by a wide smile and tears of relief as he took

Rachel from David's arms and led the way back down the steps.

Rachel's tears stopped the instant she saw that her doll was safe. Mum and Dad arrived back to find that Rachel was the only one not crying.

'It was Dave,' sobbed Auntie Sophie. 'He rescued her! Risked his own life to save her!'

David began to protest, but found himself squashed against Rachel right in the middle of a big family hug. Rachel pushed her doll into his face.

'Dabey, kiss dolly!' she commanded.

'I'm very proud of you!' said Dad, slipping an arm around David's shoulders as they walked back to The Silver Mountain Hotel. 'Thank goodness you kept your head! Uncle Richard said it was a miracle you got to her on time.'

'It *was* a miracle, Dad! A real miracle! I prayed, and God answered. I used to think He didn't listen to my prayers, but now I know He does. He helped me to do the right thing, and I'm sure He kept the decking holding together just long enough for me to get to her.'

'I'm sure you're right. If Uncle Richard or I had tried to get to her, the whole thing would probably have come down.'

'You're a star, Dave!' said Emily as she joined them. 'And I never thought I'd say that!'

Chapter twenty-five:
ANOTHER CRISIS

The last four days in Nepal were ones of great happiness for David; everyone treated him as though he was a hero, but even though he enjoyed basking in the limelight, he felt a bit of a fraud because if people knew the truth, they might not think he was so great. Even Emily, who did know part of what had really happened, couldn't find anything to fall out about.

When they made their final trip to the lakeside to do their last-minute shopping and take a rowing boat out on to the lake, David was the one Rachel wanted to sit next to.

'There will always be a special bond between you two,' said Uncle Richard as he watched Rachel reaching up for David's hand on the way back from the boats. 'And when she's older and understands what you did in Beni, then ...'

'Uncle Richard,' said David, suddenly unable to hear any more praises heaped on him, 'everyone's making out that I did something really brave ...'

'Well, you did, Dave!'

'No I didn't. Really, I didn't. If I hadn't been so horrible in the first place, she'd never have gone missing,' said David.

'Want to tell me about it?'

And so, as they walked up the hill to the shops, David told Uncle Richard every detail of how he had resented Rachel and of how jealous he was when he heard that Uncle Richard and Auntie Sophie were hoping to adopt her. He confessed how he'd let her escape the day he was supposed to be looking after her, and how she'd ended up in the water-filled drain. As he talked he wiped away the tears that were streaming down his cheeks.

'And I didn't even learn my lesson then, Uncle Richard,' he sobbed. 'I was still just as careless and horrible to her when we got to Beni! And now you know the truth, you must really hate me.'

'Dabey cry!' sobbed Rachel. Uncle Richard lifted her up and she buried her face in his neck. He balanced her on one arm so that he could put his other arm around David.

'Nothing's changed, Dave—we love you every bit as much as we always did.'

'I just wanted things to be as they were before you went away,' David blurted out. 'I guess I wanted Emily and me to be the only kids in your life. Sounds stupid, doesn't it, when you put it into words—and selfish.'

'No, it doesn't, Dave, it sounds like a boy who loves very deeply. But you know the great thing about love? There's always more. It's never-ending. Who knows, sometime in the future we might get the chance to adopt another child, and even though I can't imagine that we could love anyone as much as we love Rachel, there will be more than enough love to include somebody else.'

'What you're doing here is amazing,' said David; 'and now I've seen how some of the children live, I realize the

kind of life she might have had if it wasn't for you and
Auntie Sophie.'

'Now you're making me sound like a hero! And I
can promise you that I am anything but ...' said Uncle
Richard. 'Hey! Look at that!'

They were very close to the shops now and came across
the amazing sight of a shopkeeper trying to shoo a cow
out of his shop. The animal was pushing its nose into
all the baskets, trying to find something to eat, and was
slobbering all over the lengths of fabric. The shopkeeper
and his wife were joined by a whole group of people who
were trying, without success, to shove the cow back out
into the street. A great cry of indignation rang out as the
cow lifted its tail and left a pile of steaming dung on the
shop floor.

'Come on,' said Uncle Richard laughing, 'there's nothing
we can do to help. Let's find the others.'

They found Emily standing on the steps of the bank.

'Uncle Richard, quick—can you go in? Dad needs you,'
said Emily, taking Rachel from his arms.

'What's up?' asked David.

'There's been a landslide. The road back to Kathmandu
is closed. Mum's in a right flap! We won't be able to get
back by bus as planned.'

'So what's going to happen?' said David as Uncle
Richard sprinted up the bank steps.

Emily shrugged. 'Don't know. What if we have to walk?'

'We can't walk, Em, don't be silly. It would take
Mum about a year to walk to Kathmandu! They'll sort
something out, don't worry. The worst that can happen is
that we'll have to stay on a bit. Hey, guess what I saw on

the way back from the boat?' And he told her about the cow in the shop. As he reached the end of the story, the bank door opened and he could tell from his parents' faces that it wasn't all bad news.

'So,' explained Dad at the end of a long story about how they'd gone into the bank and heard about the landslide, and what they'd been able to sort out, 'it turns out we can fly out of here on Friday. It means going a day early, and we'll have to stay over in Kathmandu. Richard and I are going to get a taxi back to his office and sort out the details, but he doesn't think there'll be a problem. There are several flights out of here on a Friday, and we're sure to get seats on one of them.'

Chapter twenty-six:
THE LAST MORNING

Friday morning arrived all too quickly.

'All packed?' said Uncle Richard as he dropped down onto the doorstep to sit with David.

'Yeah, just about,' said David sadly.

'I'm sure it won't be long before we're home again,' said Uncle Richard.

'It seems like forever since we used to come round to your house for Sunday tea and take the football down to the park.'

Uncle Richard placed his arm gently around David's shoulders. 'Look, I ...'

Somewhere in the house there was a crash followed by the sound of Rachel crying.

'RICHARD! Quick! Can you come?' There was an urgency in Auntie Sophie's voice that made Uncle Richard jump to his feet.

'COMING! Sorry, back as soon as I can,' he said, and he dashed into the house.

David looked around the little garden and up at the surrounding buildings, trying to imprint every image on his mind. By tomorrow, this would all be a memory.

'Packing all done?' asked Dad from the doorway.

'All done,' said David.

'Your room still looks like a bomb's hit it, though.'

'It's all Emily's stuff,' said David. 'What's going on in the house? Why's Rachel crying?'

'She'd pulled something off the water filter—water going everywhere. Bit of a panic. They didn't realize she could reach it. Anyway, they're sorting it out and Emily's looking after Rachel, so that'll ensure she'll still be packing when we're due to leave!'

David laughed.

'Have you enjoyed it here?' asked Dad.

David thought for a minute before answering, 'Yeah, I have. I wasn't so sure at first. Everything was so different and everybody was just so obsessed with Rachel, but it's been great. I can't wait to tell the guys at school about everything we've done and seen. Have you enjoyed it?'

'Yes, bit of a culture shock at first, but it really opens your eyes to how people live in other places, doesn't it?' said Dad.

'And how happy they are,' agreed David. 'When we went to Beni and saw two little boys playing in the street I saw that they had no proper toys, but they were really happy.'

'So you might not be on the Xbox so much when we get back?' said Dad with a laugh.

"Spect I will—I'll have to play the game Emily bought me, won't I?' said David with a grin. 'I mean, once we get home, this will all seem very unreal, won't it, and we'll be back to our normal lives. I'll try, though. And I'll never forget this holiday. Never. It's been life-changing.'

Dad smiled and waited, thinking David was going to say more. When he didn't, he said, 'You coming in, then?'

'I'm just waiting for Uncle Richard to come back. We were halfway through a conversation.'

Dad disappeared into the house. David heard him asking Emily how she thought she was going to fit everything into her bag. David waited for what seemed a long time, and when Uncle Richard didn't reappear, he stood up, stretched and went to see what was happening inside. Auntie Sophie and Mum were mopping the kitchen floor.

'Bit of a crisis, David,' said Mum. 'Rachel's found the water filter! Uncle Richard's finding her some dry clothes. You all packed?'

David nodded and followed the sound of Rachel's squealing to the bedroom, where Uncle Richard was wrestling her into a clean T-shirt.

'As soon as this young lady is sorted I think we'd better have breakfast,' Uncle Richard said, glancing at his watch. 'Dipendra will be here with the Land Rover before we know it.'

David wandered down to the room he'd been sharing with Emily and found her trying to cram a Nepalese doll into the corner of her rucksack.

'Have you got room for this in your bag?' she asked him.

'Sorry, Em, no way am I having a doll in my rucksack!'

'It's a present for Joanna,' said Emily, 'and I can't fit it in.'

'Well, you should have bought something smaller! You'll have to leave it for Rachel.' He saw the look of exasperation on Emily's face and realized that she was almost crying. 'Oh, give it here!' He snatched it off her and unfastened his rucksack. 'But if they search my bags at the airport, you'd better admit it's yours!' He shoved the doll into his rucksack.

'I feel really sad leaving them here,' said Emily.

'I know,' agreed David, 'but it'll be all right, Em, really it will.'

Somebody shouted that breakfast was ready, so he left Emily blowing her nose and went to join everyone at the table.

Chapter twenty-seven:
A Final Surprise

David tried not to think that this would be the last meal they'd share for maybe a very long time. He accepted an extra piece of toast and was still munching it when Dad and Uncle Richard went to move the bags into the hallway, with Emily running along behind to explain about the state of her stuff.

For a few moments he was left alone at the table with Rachel. She held out her hand and he shared the last bit of toast with her.

'You're pretty special, Rachel, know that?' he whispered shyly. 'I feel very sad to be going home and leaving you here.'

Rachel reached out her hand to him and, sticky though it was, he took it and raised her little fingers to his lips and kissed them.

'Love you, Dabey,' she said, through a mouthful of toast.

'Love you too, Rachel,' he said, and kissed her on the forehead.

She pursed her lips and he laughed. 'Wait till you've finished your toast!'

'DAVID!' yelled Emily from the hallway. 'Come quick!'

He rushed into the hallway, determined that he wouldn't put any more of Emily's junk in his bag—but immediately she grabbed his arm and pulled him out of the front door.

'Quick, come on, you've got to see them!'

He ran after her as she raced through the garden and turned right on to the street.

'What are we looking at?' he yelled.

'Come on! Come on!' she urged, running even faster to the top of the street.

'There!' she panted, pointing as she slowed down. 'Look at that!'

And there, towering over the town, glinting shiny white against the clear blue sky, was the Annapurna mountain range. For the first time in two weeks the clouds had lifted. David gasped at the sight of Machhapuchhre, the fishtail mountain standing supreme above them. It was so beautiful.

'It's as if they knew it was our last day,' gasped Emily, 'as if they just had to show themselves to us before we left!'

'I can't believe the clouds could hide something so enormous!' said David. 'I never expected ... they're so beautiful, and they were there all the time! Every day when the skies were so grey and cloudy I almost didn't believe they were there.'

The rest of the family had now arrived. Rachel was pointing and clapping in Uncle Richard's arms. She held out her arms to David and he took her. She pointed at the mountains and said something to him that he couldn't

make out. He smiled at her and she rubbed her cheek
against his.

'It's such a brilliant picture of God's presence in our
lives,' said Auntie Sophie. 'We can't see Him, but we just
believe He's there, and now and again, something happens
to give us a glimpse of His glory!'

'You know what,' said Dad, 'I think I'd just like to pray
for us all while we're all together in this beautiful place.'

And that's what he did, with everyone gazing at the
mountains which were such a symbol of God's presence
and power. He prayed for God's blessing on them as
a family, for those travelling home, and especially for
those staying, and that Rachel's adoption would soon be
completed.

Chapter twenty-eight:
DAVID'S BIG DECISION

All too soon Dipendra arrived with the Land Rover and it seemed as though the clock was going twice as fast as it should do. However hard they tried to hold on to the precious moments together, time slipped away. The luggage was stashed on the roof rack and they were soon on their way to the airport.

This journey was very different from the one two weeks earlier, when it had seemed as though everyone was talking at once. Rachel was now the only one who was chattering, but even she was quiet as they pulled up in front of the airport.

Saying goodbye was horrible. David was so disappointed that he had never had a chance to finish his conversation with Uncle Richard. His heart was very heavy as he waited for his rucksack to be lifted down from the roof rack.

There were many hugs and many tears as they prepared to leave one another, not knowing when they'd meet again. Just when David thought it was the final goodbye, Uncle Richard pulled him to one side. 'I need Dave for one last minute,' he said to the others; 'we were halfway through a sentence when Rachel tried to flood the house!'

He turned to David. 'I know our calling has been tough for you. I almost think it's been as hard for you, if not harder, than it's been for us. At least we knew that we'd heard God call us to work on the mission field; the rest of you just had to go along with it.'

'Grandad finds it very hard, I think,' said David.

'I know he does. I can't wait for him to meet Rachel.'

'She'll steal his heart!' said David.

'Has she stolen yours?'

'Course she has!'

'She's going to miss you—all of you.'

'How long do you think it will be before you can come home?' David asked.

'I really don't know, Dave. So much depends on the committees we have to see and the forms we have to complete.'

'Three months? Six?'

Uncle Richard shook his head. 'I don't know, Dave. We just have to take it a step at a time.'

David nodded. 'I understand now much better than I did back home. Now I've seen what you do here and how the people depend on you and love you.'

'You've grown up a lot, Dave, even in the two weeks you've been here. I'm very proud of you!'

'Can I tell you something before we go?' David glanced over his shoulder to where everyone was waiting. 'It's really important.'

'Course you can,' said Uncle Richard, looking worried—but David smiled broadly. 'It's nothing bad. It's just that I've made a big decision and I want you to be the first to know. I've asked Jesus into my heart. It started in the church service. I was really bored and I was watching the shadows on the wall. They looked a bit like sheep, and there was one that wouldn't join up with the rest. And you know, I suddenly thought, "That's me." Some of the guys at youth group have become Christians recently—some of the cool guys—and they're different. Still cool—in fact, maybe more cool. And I thought, if that's the difference having God in your life makes, that's what I want too.'

Uncle Richard punched him lightly on the shoulder. 'Best decision you'll ever make, Dave!'

'I said the words in the church, but it wasn't until we lost Rachel in Beni that I knew that it was real and that God had answered my prayers,' said David.

'Well, I'm really proud of you, Dave, and thrilled that you've taken such an important step while you've been here! Hey, we're going to have to go—your mum's starting to panic that the plane'll go without you and she'll have to walk after all!'

They strolled over to join the others. Uncle Richard said to him, 'Tell them your news before you get home. I'll be surprised if they haven't guessed already, though. You're a different boy from the one who came here a fortnight ago.'

It was so painful to say goodbye without knowing when they would see one another again, that it was almost a relief when the time came for them to go through to the departure lounge.

'Look out for us when you take off—there's a balcony where we can watch!' yelled Auntie Sophie. 'We'll be waving! Love you!'

And then they were gone, and David's last view as the doors of the departure lounge slid together were of Rachel reaching out her arms and looking confused and upset.

The plane was tiny—David guessed it wouldn't hold more than about twenty passengers. He watched their luggage being wheeled out and loaded into the hold.

'At least we know our bags are on the plane!' said Emily.

'And everyone can see that your bag's bigger than everybody else's!' added David.

'And that's our call,' said Dad, as people around them began to stand and collect their hand luggage. They followed the small line of passengers out across the tarmac and boarded the plane. David pressed his face against the window searching for a glimpse of Auntie Sophie and Uncle Richard, but he didn't know where they would be standing and there were lots of people there. It was unbearable to think that they might take off without one last sighting of them.

The cabin doors were closed, the engines were running, and suddenly they were taxiing out towards the runway.

'It's a very small plane,' said Emily. 'I hope it'll be all right!'

'It's only a short flight, Em,' said Dad; 'no more than half an hour.'

And then they were airborne, rising above the airport buildings into the clear blue sky.

'There!' shouted David; 'there they are!'

Sure enough, they could see three well-loved, familiar figures waving for all they were worth. Rachel, wearing the same bright red dress she'd worn in Beni on the day

David had rescued her, was blowing kisses and laughing. David watched them until they were tiny dots in the distance, until he could no longer see even the airport tower—and he guessed the others were doing just the same.

Across the aisle Emily was crying and Mum was wiping her eyes. Dad smiled at him. 'All right, David?'

He nodded. He was all right. He didn't like saying goodbye either, but he knew that when he got home, life was going to be different because he was different.

'Dad, I've got something to tell you,' he said, and he began to tell Dad the story about the shadows on the church wall that had turned into the lost sheep who'd found his way back into God's family.

THE CHOCOLATE CLUB

Mary Weeks Millard

Instead of being the saddest Christmas of her life, Rosanna's big idea transforms it into a wonderful time, not only for her own family but also for two disadvantaged families.The friendship between the children develops into a club—The Chocolate Club. They have fun and adventures together as they learn to pray and see miracles happen.

Mary Weeks Millard used to work as a missionary in Africa. She now loves to write stories for younger readers.

Also available

A COBWEB COVERED CONSPIRACY

Jill Silverthorne

Martin isn't in the 'in crowd'. School's hard work—particularly as he has to be friends with bully Joe Fuller. Then Martin begins to discover who his true friends are. Together, they begin to unravel a mystery more dangerous than they could ever have imagined. Pizzas, spiders and a dog called Becker all add to the plot, as Martin finds out about the one person who he can truly rely on.

Jill Silverthorne was born and bred in South Wales. She graduated from the University of Leicester with a degree in English and went on to pursue a career in teaching.

Also available

RICHES IN ROMANIA

Rebecca Parkinson

Jenny's parents have always been able to give her everything she wants until her dad begins a new job working for a Christian charity. As Jenny struggles to come to terms with their new lifestyle, her family is invited to take part in a farming project in Romania. As Jenny and her brother David spend time in a small Romanian village, they make friends with the local children and begin to realise that friendship can break down barriers of wealth, language and culture. However, when Jenny's precious locket goes missing it seems that everything has gone wrong, until a guard, previously in the Communist regime, teaches her the secret of forgiveness and encourages her to set about putting things right in her own life.

Rebecca Parkinson lives in Lancashire with her husband and their two children. As a teacher and the leader of the youth and children's team in her church, she loves to pass the Bible stories on to others in a way that everyone can understand.

Also available

THE SECRET OF THE HIDDEN TUNNEL

Mary Weeks Millard

Matty Morris's world collapses when
her parents announce that they are
going to move to Africa and that she
will need to go to boarding school. She
is sure she won't like St Anne's, but
she quickly settles in and makes friends. Through a series of
adventures and personal challenges she and her friends make
exciting discoveries about the school's history as well as some
life-changing decisions ...

*Mary Weeks Millard used to work as a missionary in Africa. She
now loves to write stories for younger readers.*